# GIETIC

## Erotic Poems.
## Kinky Short Stories.

**Giselle writing as Gia Bella**
**Claudia Moss writing as The Siren**

**Paperback ISBN 978-0-578-00735-9**

## Acknowledge this

It's not another sad love song
It's not just another short story
And definitely not some rap lyrics
Nor jazz or blues notes.
It's not just a simple exotic piece
Spoken by an artist.

It's your mother, father, sister and
brother
Then again it's you and me.
Complete and incomplete
It's whatever it wants to be.
Understood and misconstrued
It's about one world separated
Rather than singled out hoods.
Unknown and discovered
It's what brings pleasure to us
And satisfaction to yourself.
It's about your reflection in a mirror
And the unseen similarities.
Heaven and hell
It's sometimes a devilish angel.
Give and take
It allows you to explore.
It can tell you what you already
know
And teach you what you've mastered
before.

It will take you, shake you, make
you and break you
But never will it destroy you.
It tells what your heart and soul feel
And speak what is dared to be told.
Truth and lies
It discloses what you never wanted
to know
And what you've always kept
hidden.
Beginnings and ends
It's a cycle of repeats
And a life of lessons.

It's not another sad love song
It's not just another short story
And definitely not some rap lyrics
Nor jazz or blues notes.
It's not just a simple exotic piece
Spoken by an artist.

## About we

It is not about what you can do for me
It is not about what I can do for you,
But it's about what us can do for we.
This one day you shall see.

You played your silly game with me.
I let you capture me with your touch
I allowed myself to feel with and for
you.
Sure I know what is best,
But I do not know what is worst.
I want no relationship
But maybe one with you.
Best friends or lovers,
Whatever will do.
You have it bad for another
While I seem to have it bad for you.
Emotions got the best of me
And gave me the worst of you.
Yeah, I do believe you care
But that's all that will ever be.
Our conversations get lost in meaning.
Now we're on opposite ends
I need your friendship more than ever,
However,
I am the one you say who does not
understand.
So I offer both my hands.
Because of lies you tell
You think I do the same,
But you do not know me too well.

So, I am sorry when I hurt you,
For I never meant to.
Now I promise to be no more than a real
friend
Always until the end.

It is not about what you can do for me
It is not about what I can do for you,
But it's about how we can set us free.
This one day you shall see.

**Baby call me**

Baby call me, baby call me, baby, baby
call me.
Was it that I gave you my body?
Was it that I gave you my pussy?
Or did I mesmerize you so much
With one single touch?
Am I the different woman in your
book?
Or am I the woman with that distinctive
look?

Baby call me, oh baby call me, why
don't you call me?
Maybe it's because I call too often
Or you just got me wide open.
It's the things you said to me
And the way you sexed me,
That got me behaving badly

And calling you one hundred and one
times daily.

Baby, baby, baby call me, baby I want
you to call me, come on call me.
Did I blow your mind,
And got you thinking you can't deal
with my kind?
Maybe you had me before
And don't want me anymore.
Will you let me know
So I can let this shit go?

Damn!  Baby call me, baby just call me,
baby, baby, baby call me
Let me know if there is another
Or if you just don't want to be bothered.
Don't wait too long
To let me know what I did wrong.
Let me know if I fucked up the flow
Or if you're afraid to let feelings show.

Baby, baby, baby call me.  Just call me,
baby call me
Wanna know if you're thinking of me
If you wanna be with me
Or with me have a baby,
Damn! I'm going crazy because of what
you did to me.
So baby call me, baby, baby call me, I
want you to call me, call me
Baby call me
Baby call me…

## Beyond love

Loving you like you are my unborn
child.
Adoring you like you're the Goddess of
all.
Loving you like I have nine lives.
Not limiting my body, soul and heart to
you.
Loving you like it's eternal.
Without regards to 'nothing lasts
forever'.
Loving you like it's not forbidden.
Always fulfilling every desire.
Loving you like there has never been
another.
Never missing a touch, a kiss, a caress,
an embrace.
Loving you like you are my Genesis
and Revelation.
As I am your Song of Solomon.
Loving you like it's my lesson.
Allow me to practice what I preach.
Loving you like there's no tomorrow.
With regards to our awaiting future.
Loving you like there's never a mistake.
Understanding and forgiving at all
times.
Loving you like you are my unborn
child.
Doing it unconditionally and beyond.

## Can I do what I want?

I want to trace your face,
Kiss your lips,
And caress your body.
I want to get lost somewhere
Between your soul and mine,
In that oneness, that togetherness, that
tenderness, that forever moment.
I want to feel your passion and make
you mine.
I want to have you.
I want to do you.
Can I do you for longer than a moment,
More than a minute,
Longer than one hour?
Can I do you today, tonight, tomorrow,
at midday
How about the break of dawn?
Can I, huh, can I?
Can I have you all to myself
Every time we touch,
Every time we meet,
And every time we stare?
I want to forget about the world
And remember all things about you.
I want to be your love slave one time,
And your sex slave many times.
Can I take you with me
To exotic land of gaiety?
Where I flip-flop
And become your top?
I want to turn your mind out

And turn your body in.
I want you to trust me to make you
come
Like it's your first time with one such
as me
And your last time being opened.
You know what I mean!
I want to do you
Like you want me to.
So can I do what I want?


## CRAZIE

Call me Crazie for loving you
Yeah they call me crazy
I call it love
What I think or say does not make sense
So they say I am loca
I call it passion

So you see, you are my sweet cake
Absolutely no mistake
Ummm, see you are my honey bun
Until there is definitely none

Call me Crazie for wanting you
So they call me crazy
I call it desire
Wherever I go or what I do is all with
you

Yeah they call me insane

So you see, you are my juicy yams
You're all I am
Ummm, see you are my fearless dove
In a land of lustful love

Call me Crazie for being with you
Yeah, call me crazy
Because that's all I want to do
Be with my honey bun
With you my sweet darling
Call me Crazy
Crazy for you,
Call me crazy,
Crazy it's all true
Call me crazy
Cause I'm the one for you
Call me crazy.

## ME, MYSELF AND US

You like that don't you?  Oh, yes you do!  I like it too, as a matter of fact I am enjoying this more than you do because I am the one who feels it all.  Don't you like the way my breasts sit on my chest, as if they are summoned to be yours and only yours?  I especially like them that way right now because of how turned on it makes me.  Your beauty is infinite and your sexiness is a temptress.  I can't wait to lay you down and make you feel pleasant.  I luxuriate at the current sight of your body but I just want to make you shake when you climax.  I know exactly what you want and how you want it and yes, I have been waiting all day to give it to you.  I know you've had a tough day at the office and need to relieve frustration to sleep through the night.  Tonight it's all about you and only you.  Let me run my hand from your neck over your succulent breasts and down your tummy to your private.  It's just what I want and precisely what I deserve now.  I am getting wetter and ready to take it in now but I have to be teased first.  Tickle my clit in a sexual characteristic way with the tip of your finger.  Just slowly and slightly work it up and down with the tip of the middle finger until the juices won't allow any grip but just let it slide over the clit. Then you will have to invite another into this rousing playtime. How about the little silver one which moves faster than lightning? I like that one on the very tip of my clit at level seven. You know that's the one which vibrates to three different tempos and I never have to worry about taking too long to come. It makes me feel so good that I begin to talk shit to myself, and even beg for more. I like it, I want it, so give it to me now. There it is, you horny chick. Can you bare the intensity as it vibrates against your clit in the wetness? I don't think you can because I see you move over the bed like it's driving you into a sexual madness. But don't stop darling, don't stop because I surely want to see and feel you come in that rewarding madness. I want to twirl in it with you and then lay in the aftermath and not feel able to get up. I enjoy the way it's wildly caressing my private and making me tingle with delight all over. It's definitely an erotic rapture that is immeasurable by goodness no matter how many times I go there. Can you feel it? I do! Do you want it? More than you can imagine. Will you come with me? No, I'm coming before you. But I'm not ready to come, I just want to relish in the thrill of it while I possibly can stand it all. Oh, well I want to come now and now I come so join me and release the energy. I have, I have come too! How wonderfully my body reacts when the orgasm breaks through. It's time of no control and all powers are weakened to follow the natural reaction of a sexual fulfillment with myself.

### Don't Go

If you're going baby,
Please come back soon to me.
I wish you would not be gone,
At least not for long.
When you're not near
Everything good seems to disappear.
I want you to stay
Every night and every day.
So you must really go,
This I truly know.
But before you leave
There is something I want to give.
I'm gonna tangle you up
Like a helpless buttercup,
With my mighty soul.
Then I will devour you whole.
I want you to feel my pulsating inside
As I start to ride.
Then feel me come how you like it,
On your face, where I'll sit.
I'll let you sex me again and again,
As I scream out your name in sweet
pain.
Then I'll hold you tighter,
For you to feel me release harder.
Then when I turn your mind out,
You'll let it flow with a shout.
Our love making you will always feel,
Because you know it's all real.
So, do you still wanna go,
Or do you want some mo'?

## Elevating love

I'm on cloud eight elevating to nine,
Because I got some of that
Wild Black, honey bee love.
Umm, can you feel me yet?

I'm talkin' bout that forbidden love.
The one that drips from the mouth
Down the breasts and navel
To the inner thigh.
The love that says,
"I am yours and you are mine."
The love that connects from the root of
the soul
To the tip of the fingers.

Yeah, I'm on cloud eight elevating to
nine,
Because I got some of that
Juicy, sweet, sumptuous love.
Ooh, you feel me now?

I'm talkin' bout that real thang.
So real that you can feel it
While you dream of it.
The love that curves around the buttock
To the arch in the back
All the way to the ear in one lick.
The love that makes you scream inside
And gives you silent shivers on the
outside.

Yep, I'm on cloud eight elevating to
nine,
Because I got some of that
Lip smacking, finger sucking love.
You feel the intensity, huh?

I'm talkin' bout that luscious love,
The kind that makes your mouth water
With fiery sensational desires.
Desires to taste the immaculate mind,
To eat the entire body,
And to swallow the celestial soul.
The paradisal love that satisfies
The raging sexual hunger.

That's right, I'm on cloud eight
elevating to nine,
Because I got some of that love.
That Black berry love.
That honey bee love.
That sweet, juicy love.
Some of that soul consecrated love.

I'm elevating
Elevating
Elevating

## Feel This

I want you to feel me inside of you as I
feel you within me.

Feel me when you think of painful love.
Feel me when you desire the aggressive
love.
I am it, I am that love.

Feel me reaching out to you with tears.
Feel the tears of loss and sorrow as they
flow from me to you.
I am them, I am the tears.

Feel my soul permeate through your
heart and mind.
Feel them become one to comfort the
spirit.
I am that, I am the spirit.

Feel my tense body fill with passion.
Feel the passion that your physical
being wants from mine.
I am she, I am the being.

Feel my fingers walk over your face
through your hair.
Feel mine escape through your fingers.
I am those, I am these fingers.

Feel my life sink into yours.
Feel your life plunge into mine.

I am it, I am our life.

Feel me when you feel this.

## Gutt feeling

Chills down my spine
Bones shivering within
Goose bumps running over my skin
Frightened butterflies in my gut.
All this at 3:03 in the morning
While I'm under a warm blanket.
Could it be because of you?
Yeah, because you are selfish.
Could it be because of love?
Yeah, since you make it seem so true.
Could it be what you do to me?
Yeah, it's what you put me through.

Chills down my spine
Bones shivering within
Goose bumps running over my skin
Frightened butterflies in my gut.
All this at 4:27 in the morning
While I'm under a warm blanket.
Could it be because of you?
Nah, it's because of me.
Could it be because of love?
Nah, it's the way I love you.

Could it be what you do to me?
Nah, it's what I allow you to do.

# COMPLEX PLEASURES

She stared Dalia in the eyes and said, "I don't love you anymore!" So easily she said it. So relieved she sounded after only the longest two years together.

Two more years have passed and Dalia still loves her. She has never stopped thinking of her and the love they shared and could still be sharing. She glanced at the waiter and then looked down to fasten the button which came undone because of her thirty-four C cup fitting into a medium size shirt. After all she had to give it to them just how they like it. He smiled and she smiled back. 'Pervert', she thought. The date was obviously not going as she'd plan. How could she not be attracted to this young, vibrant, chatty, chocolate sister? Her hair was straight and silky down to her neck, which lead to her slender arms spouting out of a spaghetti-padded top that exposed her mid-cut cleavage. She seemed clueless. Wait, she was clueless. As she went on about something, Dalia noticed another. She had a mole on her left breasts, a beauty mark and was it ever the most beautiful mark she'd noticed on anyone. She wanted to lick it, suck it and maybe bite it. She looks up at her slightly crooked smile showing just enough teeth and teasing with the tip of her tongue exposed. Shit! Dalia smiled back. More conversation after dinner and now Dalia was attracted to her. She was petite, a size four perhaps, with a physique toned and healthily maintained, and her skin seemed more than just smooth. Despite being chatty and clueless that she was not being listened to, Dalia could surely fukc her. She looked good enough to take it all night. Dalia imagined being on top of her with her hands around her neck and her 9" strap-on in her pussy as she called her a slut. She wanted to slap her apple bottom red and make her beg for more. She wanted her to be her nasty little sex slave just for the night. She'd never been with anyone romantically since the break up. Dalia didn't want to be alone but she didn't want to be in love either. She wanted to ask her to come home with her to exchange fukc faces but instead she looked at her between the eyes and asked, "I just want to hold you, can we go to my place?" Little to her surprise the chick said yes without hesitation. 'Freak', she thought. Three hours after the getting to know each other conversation they began to make out. In the living area on the floor of Dalia's high rise apartment over looking the highway and city lights their bodies where explored by each other. Dalia caressed her clit and the inside of her pussy with two fingers making her moan with satisfaction. She played with her pussy, sucked on her nipples, and kissed her until she climaxed. Now it was her turn to be pleased and she wanted it right. It had been one month since she got some head and she wanted it now. She gently guided the girl's head to her pussy. She wanted her to eat it, suck it, lick it and make her cum. Now much to her surprise she ate that pussy right. It was like she knew what Dalia liked, how she liked it and when to do it. She licked her clit over and over after she tongue fukced her and sensually twisted her lips around it. She was coming, Dalia was going to nut. She did! She came! Pleased with her performance the girl slowly eased her body over Dalia's and rested on her full chest. "I knew exactly what you needed and it wasn't complex and I still know what pleasures you desire." Could this be the end of letting that old shit go or the beginning of discovering something new? 'Damn', Without any other thoughts Dalia fell asleep.

## How do I?

We were so damn strong for so damn
long.
I thought nothing would break or
damage us.
Now I am just lost in meaning,
where I fail to understand what
happened
or what went wrong so damn quickly.

So Baby tell me
How do I let go?
How do I get to where you are,
Happy and fulfilled without me?
How do I not reminisce about us
when I hear a love song?

So honey tell me.
How do I let it be?
How do I leave the memories behind
and throw out the memoirs?
How do I heal this wound
that is deeper than I can dig?

So my love tell me.
How do I forget?
How do I erase the best
and most important part of my life?
How do I love another
the way I love you or you love her?

So my darling tell me.
How do I go on?
How do I stop the tears
and live in laughter again?
How do I pull it together
and keep you as a friend?


So my lover tell me.
How do I move on?
How do I forget the plans we had
and make others with another?
How do I get my life back
without you in it?

So tell me my sweetheart.
How do I get over this?
How do I become whole again
without my entire being?
How do I share with another
without comparing to you?

So tell me my dear.
How do I?
How do I become like you,
NOW?
How do I stop loving you?

### If one day

If I have one day with you,
I will get to know you.
Tell you I first liked your smile,
I will find out what makes you happy
And keep you that way for the longest
while.

If I have one day with you,
I will get to know you better.
Tell you secrets and find out yours.
I will massage your body
And receive your spirit.

If I have one day with you,
In love with you I will be
Confess it to you and the world.
 I will treat you like a queen,
And always remain loyal.

If I have one day with you,
I will make love to you like I'm your
last
And sex you down fervently.
Fukc you till we both break into sweats
And make love to you like I'm your
first.

If I have one day with you,
I will love you at every moment
And cherish every hour.
I will love you till the end of that day

And to the beginning of the next
lifetime.


## LOVE

Love, love, love
What a motherfucker!

It will have you doing things.
Things that are immoral,
Things that are untrue,
Things that aren't loyal.

It will have you forgetting people.
Forgetting friends,
Forgetting trust,
Forgetting YOU!

It will have you lying to her
And him lying to you,
Your friends lying to each other,
And you lying to yourself.

It will have you complicating things,
Destroying relationships,
Turning your best friend into an enemy
And an enemy into your best friend.

It will motivate you
Then leave you uninspired,

Giving you the support you need
While taking away your strength.

It will give you rainy days
And sunny nights.
Times you will remember for a lifetime
And times you always want to forget.

It will have you wanting more
But getting less,
And have you giving more
Of your worst.

It will turn a frown into a smile
And turn laughter into tears.
Your face can radiate like a sun
While your soul reflects an eclipse.

It won't tell you when it's right
And it never tells you when it's wrong.
But it will show you
How to turn a wrong into a right.

It will set your mind at ease
And let your spirit be free.
But your body, your temple
May be enslaved and bruised.

It will teach you
But will never be taught by you.
One lesson from it can last a lifetime.
But one relationship with it can last a
moment.

It can change you at anytime,
And create a new you every time.
No matter how many times or ways you
experience it,
It will always be LOVE!

Love, love, love
What a wonderful motherfucker!

# ONE LAST TIME

Theopus was sure he would never give his entire being to another man again. That bastard didn't have the guts to tell him that he was married before they got serious. Shortly after Theo gave him his heart he decided to go back to his wife. Theo felt every negative emotion draining from within to his solid exterior, but he could not let it get what was left of him. It had now been three months since he last saw Rich and Theo thought for sure that he would be ready to socialize if not try out the dating scene. So he decided to do it alone without any of his pushy friends who would try to hook him up with nearly everyone they thought to be handsome. Some part deep inside still desired Rich's sexy chocolate firm body against his, but he knew that he should not call him at all. As Theo reached for his coat, the phone rang. He looked at the caller identifier and decided the best thing to do was ignore it and head out for an entertaining night. The machine picked up, but no message was left. Then the phone rang a second time and when he reached for it the machine picked up again. He waited for a moment and when the phone did not ring again he walked out the door. Before he could pull out of the driveway his cellular rang, he looked at the screen and thought what if something is wrong.

"This is Theo," he answered the call.

"You know who this is boy. Why weren't you picking up?" Rich's voice came through dominating.

"Not home. Wha' you want Richard?" Theo did not want to give him another second to lead the conversation, "you!" Rich responded overly confident.

"Richard, I don't have time for your tomfoolery and bullshit so unless you have something meaningful to ask or say - do not call me," he was sure that now the he had control of the call as he added, " besides I am busy."

With child like confidence, Rich took back over the conversation, "No you're not, you're not busy. You're never too busy for me."

Theo had enough of is ignorant self-importance, "Look Richard," and before he could even get another word out Rich interrupted, "Stop calling me Richard! You know me better, you know me best, you know me Theo" Theo heard a faint tremble in his voice. He wanted to ask what was wrong, he wanted to know why he phoned, "Okay Rich, what is it?" whether he wanted to hang up or not his heart would not allow it.

"Will you get out of the car and talk to me," Rich desperately needed Theo.

Startled by his demand Theo responded with bittersweet questions, "Are you fukcing spying on me? Richard, what the hell is wrong with you," he kept expressing soulful hurt, "you don't call me for any other reasons but you, you, you, your problems, your issues, your this and thats. I am so tired of being there for your sorry ass and now you want to ruin my night. Rich you can't" before he could go on Rich reached over then opened Theo's car door and swung it exposing a red faced, pale angry man. Theo could not bring himself to make a sound as he stopped and gawked with delight and regret.

"I am sorry," Rich was more than apologetic he was miserable, "I do love you. I don't want to lose you or leave you. I don't want to recreate what we had, I want to expand who we are, together."

Theo could almost hear his heart beat but almost wasn't good enough.

"We are not going to make a scene out here, so can we please go inside," Rich begged with misery still lingering in his eyes. Without questions or comments Theo led the way until he closed the door once they were in the apartment. Rich released his being on the couch then Theo sat on the sofa waiting for him to begin speaking. The love in his heart would not stand still while Rich hurt so his lips began to move and the words sounded, "What's wrong Rich?" then his mind took over, "what are you doing here in the middle of the night? What do you want?"

"I want you to listen," Rich beckoned. "I want you to know," he paused to control his emotion and focus his thoughts. "She and I are over." He knew that Theo would cut in so he went on without giving him time to, "I told her I was in love with someone else. I told her I was in love with a man. I told her your name and I told her why."

Theo's eyes ran wild as his mind wondered if this was the moment he was longing for and his heart began to race with fear because he knew it could or very well could not.

Rich continued as he eased himself to the sofa, "I want to give us more than a chance. I want to give us more than a try. I want to give us a life." He reached over and touched Theo's hand, "I want more than love with you Theo!" he let Theo feel the intensity as he clinched onto his arm. He knew that Theo desired him as much as he hungered for him, therefore, there was no more time to waste. Rich brusquely leaned over and kissed him as if he'd been the one waiting for his return. As arrogant as Rich was Theo knew he had to receive him now then fuss later. He allowed his tongue passed his lips and beyond his teeth to tangle with his tongue to speak a language better than French. Rich could not contain himself as he had not had sex in over nine weeks and wanted it from Theo now. He aggressively pulled and threw off his shirt then began to passionately suck on each nipple causing Theo to release a moan more sensual than that of a woman completely elated. After exposing his slender, still nude body showered with kisses and tenderly caressed by a man Rich grabbed his erect penis.

"Rich I know you don't want to and you" without letting him continue in pity, Rich readily and firmly pressed his lips against the top of Theo's penis. He then opened his mouth taking in his rawness as deep as he could stand it. Again without hesitation Rich knew what Theo wanted and he sucked and softly retched on his stiff dick with a steady hand and jaw movement that brought the young man to the highest height. Theo was not only in amazement because Rich had never performed fellatio before but also because he knew every blood vessel on the dick. He knew he had to do more than return the favour but much to his surprise the bombastic bastard wanted to only please him tonight. Rich was still facing Theo as he unhurriedly brought him down to his dick. Before he slid into his asshole he stuck three fingers into his own mouth then with that saliva rubbed it onto the opening of Theo's ass. Theo felt wholesome and accepted Rich now more than ever into his heart, body and soul. As Rich slithered into him they both knew it was now time to fukc. Theo thrust his body onto Rich who filled him up with pure pleasure and back and forth they went in rapture like untamed beasts. With their bodies glowing in sweat Theo was ready to climax but wanted Rich to come also and before he could tell him he was coming, he felt it from Rich. They both released with completeness and full satisfaction. Theo, then, really understood why he could never love another man, "you only get one more chance and one last time to love and be loved by me."

At that instance, Rich knew he'd found himself and had made the right decision to pursue love, for had he stayed with his wife then it would have been a choice.

**Love making love**

It's a passion that burns within
Stronger than a brush fire,
And the love comes out
Flowing faster than Trafalgar Falls.

Contentment when exchanging bodily
fluids
And finding ecstasy at the same time.
Creating undying moments
That surpass flying above cumulous
clouds.

It's whispers of kind nothings through
nights
That give meaning to love,
And words of comfort spoken
To offer understanding of each other's
spirits.

Eye catching sentences
Which breathe out souls of pure
happiness,
With tangled body shadows over the
walls
That explore into lighted darkness.

It's sharing the minds without regards
To losing oneself in thoughts,

While volunteering the body
To be taken and satisfied at the same
time.

Like finding yourself in her
Everytime your lips meet,
And overcoming failure when your
touch
Is responded to with breath sweeping
moans.

It's more than saying I love you
When your fingers are locked together,
By letting your bodies speak of love
When you are close enough to feel your
heart beats.

Never second guessing yourself
Because you truly know where you are
headed,
To a place of gratitude that magnifies
Larger than an outburst of climax.

It's when you are in love
And are with the one you love,
There is nothing more powerful
Yet more mind destructive than in love
making love.

## Love Wave

Well here is a love wave
Heading your way,
You think you're brave,
Baby not today.
It comes unexpectedly,
Making you change you,
To no longer be free
Not a life partner but a boo.

Are you with me?

That wave takes you by surprise
Making you believe saying "baby I'm
true"
Taking you on a continuous rise
Until one day saying "I think I love
you"
Knowing that after "I think?"
You should probably be on separate
ways
You stick around just letting that one
blink
Hoping that ahead are better days.

That love wave will take you on
drowning journeys
But you think you can handle it
Because of excuses and apologies
Even if it's all bullshit.
The pleasing passion of it all
Will have you feeling that it's strong

And no matter what you can't fall
Especially when it's bound to last long.

It will have your knees shaking and
body weak
Day or night and when your think of
that loving
Because you know how you like that
lick
Even if you should not let it happen.
The wave is guaranteed to make you
wet
And keep you ready to go
And always hot and ready to get
What you know should be a no.

Then one day when you least expect
After you have gotten all caught up
Without a sign and without slightest
respect
The wave will take you down not
making it able to get up.
The love wave will then be too cool
Making you shiver and just be
Another one reeled in and made a fool
After changing you from being free.

Were you with me?

So next time that love wave hits
Don't stick around long
And don't even try to surf it
Because you just might drown.

But when that love boat
Comes for you
Get in but keep the life float
Because another love wave might try to
break through.

**Miles away**

I miss you.

I miss you like a forehead kiss
At the break of dawn.
Like an amazed silent stare
Knowing you are the one.

I miss lying on your left side
Knowing you are right there.
Feeling your embrace throughout the
night
As we lovingly reach for each other
during sleep.

I miss the soft way you speak
And confident way you act.
When you hold and rub my hand
And affectionately make adoring love to
me.

I miss the midnight conversations

And midday fukcs.
The way we get to know each other
Understanding what we need and want.

I miss you more than the day would
miss the sun
And the night would miss the moon.
The ways we got lost in each other's
soul
And simply say I love yous.

I miss you when you're not here
Hoping and believing that you will
return.
I miss you when you're gone
Knowing that it won't be too long.

Still missing you.

## SECRET AFFAIRS

Cienna slowly sipped her drink as she observed others doing the same across the round bar. She wondered if most of them were there for the same reason as her. She wanted to get laid. As erotic thoughts evaded her mind, she didn't even notice that the seat next to her been occupied. As she turned around to request another drink, she faintly heard his voice.

"Pre-occupied with deep thoughts?" his curiosity aroused her.

"Hello to you, too, and why do my thoughts concern you?" Cienna really wanted to know.

The gentleman smiled with his eyes; "maybe they're the same as mine."

She couldn't bare it any longer as she sensually leaned over and whispered, "would you like to find out?" And before her lips closed her tongue made it's way to his ear lobe, he let out a private moan for her ears only. He wanted to find out.

So began the simply introduction, "I'm Eryck with a 'y' and a 'k'"

"I'm Cienna, like the vehicle, but with a 'c'."

"I would love to take you out of here and somewhere more intimate" he sounded more demanding than proposing.

She desired some place that no one would find them, "I have a place in mind. Why don't you follow me outta here" she knew the perfect spot, "it's walking distance!"

He was surprised, and to himself he wondered how many times she'd probably done this before, yet he let her lead. He followed her through an exit door in the back of the bar, down a few steps and into a cellar type door.

"Where exactly are we going and how do you know about this spot?" His words represented his skeptic mind.

With confidence in her voice and attitude Cienna opened the door, "it's my cousin's place and this is his office, but don't worry because he's outta town for a couple more days." Before she could give him a chance to think she went on, "I am the only other person besides his off duty manager who has a key."

They paused, they hesitated but knew what each other wanted so without rules and regulations they moved on. It was like they could read each other's mind. Their lips never once touched each other's but they certainly kissed over a dozen places. Cienna just wanted him inside of her as deep as he could get or she could stand it. Eryck dynamically grabbed her ass as he pulled her towards him. With a skirt on, she made it just easier for him to remove her thong as she viciously unfastened his belt and his pant exposing an erect magnum dick. She melted with satisfaction before they began. As he kept one hand on her left breast he wildly rushed two fingers into her wet pussy. He could feel his dick throb with approval.

"More, more fingers baby," she begged with pleasure as he inserted two more causing her moan to deepen. "You want this pussy sucking on your big ass dick, don't you?"

"Hell fukcing yeah!" Eryck had a rush of sexual fever run through his body.

He vigorously turned her around, "just turn the fukc around bitch and take that dick like a ho."

Cienna felt her pussy drip at the end of his words as she put her back into it while he penetrated her.

"Oooh, that feels good, huh? You like the way I'm wet? Wait till I start riding you" her voice was faint yet alive.

It felt like an adulterated goodness that would remain sacred to a man and a woman wanting it the same way at the same time. They felt wholesome and alive.

"Fukc me hard and deep, you bastard! I want to feel you so far up in my gut that I beg for mercy." Her demanding yet sexy tone turned him on even more.

"Oh yeah baby! Be careful what you wish for. You know you probably can't handle all of that shit," and before he could go further Cienna interrupted him with her movements. She pulled herself away from him, turned around and looked him in the eyes, "get on your back on that couch," as he moved with a delayed reaction she placed her tiny hands on his chest and forced him onto his back. She was charmed that she got him so aroused as she glanced at his hard, erect penis.

"Don't just look at it woman. Get on the damn dick and show me what you can do." Eryck wanted to stare in her face as she took it all in. Cienna gracefully swung her right leg over his body and moved smoothly down onto his hard cock.

"Oooh, Oooh yeah! That shit is better than ever" as she began to ride him with flexible hips and a thirsty pussy he wanted more of her. His penis was comfortably molded in her hot, wet pussy as she rode back and worth. They both wanted it faster, so he grabbed her by the waist and positioned her to take it as he lifted her in and out over him.

As he rammed into her harder with every stroke, Cienna enjoyed the sprinkles of erotic pleasure that ran through her aesthetic body.

"You're gonna make me cream over your dick baby," he heard the rush of an approaching orgasm in her words.

"Fukc! That pussy is so damn good. I'm gonna cum too baby! I want to feel you tighten around my dick." He was holding back, "baby cum, baby, baby cum."

"I'm coming, I'm coming! Oooh yes! That's that good ass dick. Shit!" before she could add anything Eryck followed through, "Hell fukcing yes!" as he squeezed her down onto him so she could feel him flow deep in her.

They barely exchanged words as they fixed themselves and headed out the back door. Eryck was a gentleman despite his sexual encounters, therefore, he walked her to her vehicle and made sure she locked the doors as he watched her drive off. Cienna walked through her front door feeling utterly satisfied and totally worn out. She made her way to bed and when she was all settled in, she heard her husband pull in the garage. She pretended to be asleep as she listened to his every considerate motion.　Cienna looked at the clock before he got into bed.

She gently propped up her head and politely asked, "Did you stop to get something to eat honey?"

Assured that he did not wake her he responded, "I surely did.　You should be tired baby, I know you had a long evening."　He eased into bed and drew his wife to lay on his chest.　"I really had a good time tonight.　I love you baby."　He held her like he'd never let go.　"I love you, too, Eryck, with all my heart."

## Mind Game

With them you can play.
With moi you are limited.
Not a bad thing,
But not a good thing.
For now you see I know your game,
Simply because I am the same.
Now should we be
More than friends,
And play each other,
Or play together?
Maybe we should just continue
What has already begun.
Maybe we should discontinue,
What is yet to come.
I love your style
As much as you love mine.
You like my wit
As much as I like yours.
Together we are more than excellent,
But less than perfect.
We know how much we need each
other
And how well we are together,
But seem to turn to another.
The reasons we don't even know
Especially when mentally
They do not stimulate the flow.
This nasty little game shall we play no
more.
I say come to me darling
And let us explore.

With them I can play.
With toi I am limited.
Not a bad thing,
But not a good thing.
Ok, forget the other stuff,
Let's just at least fukc!


**One down...**

Eyes to eyes
Wondering what wants, desiring,
craving
My body, my mind, my tenderness, my
pussy.

Hand running up thigh
Making me high, wet, submit
My womanhood, my fluids, my
orgasms, my clit.

Lips against lips
I'm about to twirl those hips, wind and
grind
Against yours until you feel the heat.

Tongue on nipples,
Becoming hard, teasing, lashing
Causing vagina walls to race against
heart beat.

Fingers fukcing,
One, two maybe three, deeper, harder
Pleasant pain, mind blowing orgasmic
ride.

Face into wetness,
Performing at best, throbs, moans
Allowing it all to be released from
within.

You holding me,
Us understanding we, complete,
togetherness
Knowing it's just one down…heading
to infinity.

**Threesome**

I lay at nights thinking of you.
I lay tonight thinking of you.
Masturbating right now thinking of you,
No, no…fukcing myself thinking of
you.
What is it that you do to me?
What have you done to me?
I cannot reply
So I don't even try.
I just continue to do what I do,

Thinking about how much I need you.
Hell, thinking about how much I hunger
for you.
I don't even want to be through.
Oh, shit…I don't even want to cum.
I just wish you weren't gone.
Come on baby,
I just want you to savor the honey fluids
Of my hot, wet pussy.
Nah…I need you to eat me,
Yeah…I need you to fukc me.
I can't stop coming,
So I will keep flowing.
I can't help the way you make me feel
Even if I know the deal.
So what? You're not here with me
Next time around she'll know where
you'll be.
So what? You're with her somewhere,
Next time around she'll know you're
here.
Damn, I wish now you were with me,
In sweet ecstasy.
So, I'll wait my turn to punish her,
By letting you fukc me.

**To say I love you**

I want to say something to you
I want to tell you something that's true.

I like the way you make me feel
I admire how you keep it real.
I dig you.

I appreciate the time we share
And know how much you care.
I respect you.

I want to say something to you
I want to tell you something that's true.

I like the way you inhale my thoughts
And exhale them with undefiled
passion.
I want you.

I more than enjoy the way you touch me
tenderly
And hold me strongly.
I like you.

When you give comfort to me
And keep me happy.
I praise you.

I want to say something to you
I want to tell you something that's true.
I love you.

# INVOLVED BACHELOR

His name is Jezz Boat, smooth and easy-going like a jazz musician yet hotter than an under wear model. He is taller than six feet two inches and built to outdo any Olympian. With golden brown eyes and light brown curly hair, cleanly shaven face and a straight pearl white smile, strongly sculptured visage with eyebrows well tamed, he is the beauty of the Gods and Goddesses. And down there? He is beyond blessed! The problem is that Jezz knows it. It's a problem alright because he is an arrogant, self righteous, unkind, insensitive, selfish, pompous son of a bastard. He doesn't know how to keep his dick down and mouth shut when it comes to getting the ladies. Jezz is the kind of guy who would try it all. He had been with the freakiest women to the twenty-seven year old virgin. Almost every weekend he was in some bed with a different girl.

There's Naydine, the super freak, fabulous, young and talented actress. She is exceptional. She lets him hit it in any position possible. She especially loves it doggy style. Sometimes, she begs for him to nut in her mouth. She loves to taste the juices of his manhood right after it's been in her wet and throbbing pussy. Nadine is the kind of girl without limitation. She is more than liberal. She even has sex with women and multiple partners. There's no way she can be Jezz' girlfriend. There's Raechel, who is the freak. She is classy, sexy and a well-groomed businesswoman. She wants nothing more than sex from Jezz. She enjoys dominating him in bed since it makes her feel powerful and superior. Raechel gets it when she wants it and how she desires it. She doesn't care to suck his dick and she can give a damn if he eats her out. If you let her tell it, she'll say she just wants to nut off his long, thick ass dick. Jezz knows he would not be able to maintain any steady relationship with a woman who wants to wear the pants in their relationship. Then there is Ticha. She is tender, quiet, sensual and lovely in almost every way, yet there is a part of her that is all so carefree. She knows what Jezz is up to; therefore, she refuses to care. That's smart enough to not allow herself to be hurt. She enjoys being with him sexually, he satisfies her and that is enough to keep him around. With every experience in bed with him she gets a better understanding of her desires. She mostly likes to suck his dick because when she performs the best fellatio he may not need the pussy. That is pure pleasure to them both. His large penis in her dripping vagina, moving in and out makes her feel passion and come with complete contentment. Although Jezz finds time with Ticha reassuring, he is absolutely not ready to settle down.

Jezz is best friends with the ultimate girl. She is Jada. She has the name of a model, film star and the brains of it all. Just imagine the female Jezz without all the sex stories. She is slender with elegant legs and perky full breast cups. She has a smile light enough to brighten a room and just wide enough to notice her eyes do the same. Jada and Jezz have been friends since the eleventh grade and during college, although at separate schools, they managed to remain friends and grow closer. Now in their late twenties and professionally successful, one of the few things missing is a romantic relationship for both. Often, Jezz suggests they hook up, but Jada dismisses the idea with general comments about his promiscuous, unpredictable sexual behaviour, which would get him in trouble. She certainly is not willing to risk her reputation, life and friendship with him for a romantic relationship that may not work. Jada has nothing to do tonight and doesn't feel like being alone so as usual she hangs out with Jezz. Spending time with him helps Jada forget her issues. Tonight she promises not to let Jezz get her drunk, because the last time she did she could not make it to work the following day. Halfway into the night they both get pissy ass drunk. Since Jezz' place is closer, Jada decides to spend the night as usual. Tonight is different, however. She wants to try some of that dick that all the women rant and rave about. The dick that makes them go mad and even have driven some to stalk it. Jezz stared with awe, is she really going to give it to him? They start by kissing, but that they barely do. Jada just wants to fukc. Damn! Big dick motherfukcer, she thinks to herself with a sudden urge to gag on it. She grabs it with a sensual force and brings her mouth to it. She teases the head, the tip of his dick then she slowly drives her mouth over his hard prick. Oh, my! Jezz can't believe it, not only is Jada sucking his dick, she's going deep throat and doing a damn good job. He takes control and by her shoulders abruptly brings her up to him. With eyes to eyes and dick to pussy they meet. Jada lets out the sexiest moan of sweet sexual pain as he continues to ease in her. Oh, that dick feels so good and so right to her. Ah, that pussy feels so wet and just right to him. Missionary. Doggie style. Woman on top. Woman on top riding from the back. Woman on top in a split. Woman on top fukcing man. Come you bastard, come and shoot that cum up in my mouth. You damn nasty slut, get down there and suck that cum juice. Thoughts they had and words that didn't need to be exchanged since their bodies spoke to each other. An hour later Jezz turns to her in his arms and tells her that for all the times he talked shit to her, she actually showed him she was the shit. Another hour passes and continuous conversation Jada whispers to Jezz, "I love you darling, but I cannot see me as your girl. You have always been involved with too many women; therefore, you only know how to be a bachelor and I don't want to be the one you make your first love." He holds her tightly and decides to never let go.

**Touched by a caress**

Felt for life
The softest most passionate touch
I embraced from you
As you softly knew
How to please me.
        Indefinitely.

In your simple caress
You had me.
        In bliss,
        In fear,
        In love,
        In confusion.

Thirsty fingers yet unselfish
As they stroked my body
They offered pleasure with pure
satisfaction.
Enthused to know you can please,
My heart is ready to love with ease.
        Freely.

In your warm stroke
You had me.
        Lose my mind,
        Find my passion,
        Give you me,
        Take you in.

You permeated through my body to my
soul

All in one forbidden touch.
I wish to give you more of me.
I wish to have more of you,
And the touch that transcends being
caressed
Eternally.


## Undecided

Tempted to leave it all behind
Afraid to let it all go.
Certain to make it alone,
Unsure to be alone.

Loving and wanting to be loved,
And hating every part of it.
Turning suspicions into dreams,
And dreams into accusations.

Understanding the difference,
But not embracing the similarities.
Desiring each other to fullest,
Yet straying from the touch of ecstasy.

Wanting it all together,
But choosing opposite directions.
Forgetting the best,
And remembering the worst.

Tempted to leave it all behind
Afraid to let it all go.
Sure to be alone,
Uncertain to make it alone.


## While Reminiscing

I woke up this morning
With a smile wider than the ocean of
love,
I actually had time to fix breakfast,
Make the bed,
And to get dressed.
But oh-oh
It's not time for work yet.
Look what you've done to me.

So I get back under the covers fully
dressed
Reminiscing about the previous night.

The way you sucked on me in every
way and everywhere.
And when your soft, luscious lips
hugged mine.
MY-TOP-CAME-OFF
The way you licked my ears and neck
And bit my nipples
While you caressed my breasts and
grabbed my ass.

MY-PANTS-WERE-NEXT
When your tongue was tangled with mine
As you tasted the saliva of my soul
Oh, damn it felt so good, so fu…..good.
MY-BRA-AND-PANTIES-WERE-GONE
As I kept feeling you between my legs again
Making sure I felt the sensation of every stroke,
Against my Cute Little Intimate Tongue.
OH-YEAH-I-STARTED-TO-TOUCH
The way you clutched me tightly
Because you knew I was coming in ecstasy
And would try to break free.


CLIMAX
RELEASE
RELAX
Damn, I did it again
Reminiscing about last night.

Now it's time to rush to work,
But Its ok
'Cause I'm gonna have a lovely day.

## UNCOVERED

I stand in the kitchen where I used to cook for you, for us and then a stupid love song comes on the radio which reminds me of even more. I can see myself standing there through the dining room mirror looking at what used to be. *You picked me up gracefully and sat me on the counter top allowing me to open my legs as you fit in closely. You kissed me seductively as you made your way to remove my panties. From my lips to my breasts, you made me feel attractive in a T-shirt in the kitchen. From my breasts to my pussy, you had dessert before dinner.* I stared deeper in the mirror attempting to recognize my face as I saw you licking your lips complementing me on dessert.

So I am driving going nowhere, I think, then before I turn down a familiar street I hear your voice bantering and tempting. I smile and feel your touch. *I can't remember where we were going, but we weren't pressed to get there. Your fingers inquisitively found themselves uncovering my skirt. I sat in the vehicle with my private slightly exposed caring, but not bothered with who saw. I felt one finger in and my left hand tightened on the steering wheel, next I felt another finger and my right hand grabbed on tighter. They thirstily looked for juices by making their way in and out of me and at one instance, I became totally focused about the gas and brake pedal. You ask me if I like it or want you to stop, but all that came out while I was concentrating on the road was, 'uh-huh'.* I pull up next to a truck at a stoplight and notice that he is smiling a little too much. At that moment I realize that I smiled hard first and he just happen to see me.

I feel sick and need to take a bath instead of a long shower. I start the water and watch as it mixes with the bath beads. A bubble burst and I see you come out of it, stepping into the tub. *You had a long drive home and your body and feet ached. I understood. I watched as you got into the tub looking more beautiful than ever whether you were tired or not, your body remained exquisite. As I bathed you, I thought of things I would like to do to you and without a second thought I felt the water bordering my body while I traced my fingers around yours. Closer than ever, you kissed me with an energy from within. Your neck was more than inviting, it propositioned me to kiss it while my fingers crept down your half submerged body and began to touch you in a place sacred only known by you and myself.* I heard every moan distinctly and before long I could feel them coming as I felt you releasing the aches. I lay my head back and turn off the water to relax as I wish memories away.

It's 05:17 in the morning and while everyone around me is sleeping, I am up. My only reason could be that I had an awful dream or just need you. I turn over to reach for you. *As I slept on my side with my back facing you, I felt you touching and caressing me making me feel heavenly. I fell into deeper sleep, however, I felt you at some point affectionately place your body over mine while spreading my legs to fit your body on top and into mine. My body wanted to sleep, but my heart and mind begged for you to keep going. With every soft kiss you blessed me with, I grew to love you more. As I laid in love, pretending to fight you for sleep, I uncovered your hunger for me at the break of dawn. The stroke of your hand and body against mine had me wake in wetness anticipating you inside of me, loving me, tasting me, finger fucking me and never letting go.* I reach as far as I can and bring the covers up closer then decide to go back to sleep until the sun comes up.

It's been a season and I wonder if you remember me last. *I knew I needed to please you beyond utopia so you would never forget and always remember. As I watched you lying next to me, all I could think of was giving you what you'd given and more. I covered your sweet body with kisses to make up for messing up our first kiss. Your artistic body beckoned me to show no mercy and give you exactly what you wanted and have you just how I desired. I touched you in places I ignored before and gave you greatness in moments. Pure satisfaction ran you wild when you told me I had given you the best head ever. I knew it was, for I had been studying you my lover, I had gotten to know you better and listened closer. I found you that day I thought as I uncovered myself in your arms. I loved you to the moon and back and back again.* There's nothing left to uncover except that true love really never dies.

## Without...With

Let me begin by saying I love you

Without you I fade away,
Even on paper.
With you I am reborn
And find individuality.

Away from you I vanish,
Into a condensed, polluted world.
Near you I become
A pillar of existence.

Allow me to continue loving you

Without you I lose my spirit,
Which may crucify my being.
Again with you I am whole
Finding reason to survive.

Apart from you, I am lost
And find my soul buried.
But with you, I gain a path
Paved through it all.

Let me end here while you still love me.

## You are my

You're my breeze on humid days
And you quench my nightly droughts.
I can feel and taste you.

You're my bitter-sweet-sour pain
A healthy, lustful addiction.
You're my pleasure at all cost.

You're my madness within a twist of
sanity,
And my picker upper when I fall.
Your strength runs through me.

You're the escape when I can't find me
And my journey to an unknown
destination.
Until the end, I'll desire you.

You're my lost and gained treasure,
Absolutely priceless.
 With you I'm madly in love.

### You got Me, you!

Not my first and maybe not my last
But, oh, that would be fine to always
have you.
I still remember the gentlest most
sensual caress.

Oh, yeah, touch me there.
The days you studied my anatomy
For the night you pleased me.
You devil, you!

You just knew how to touch me,
Fill me with your tongue and fingers.
You bad ass, you!

The stroke of experience
And knowledge against my pussy
Taking me to lovely utopia.
You tease, you!

Your mouth on my vagina whipping my
clit.
Your fingers touching and fukcing.
You woman, you!

Learn, give and take from me
But taste the syrup of life from my
sugar walls.
You shall not forget the gentlest most
sensual woman.

## You to me to you

You love me
It's better
In every way
And every day.

You mock me
It's worse
Not so often
Yet not so softly.

You spell me
It's bounded
The four letter word
Most kind and overwhelming.

You know me
It's broken
Misinformed about my true,
Only myself to blame.

You share me
It's mended
Not keeping me all to yourself,
But wanting me all to your desires.

You almost me
It's similarities
That I point out to us
Yet keep hidden from myself.

You give me

It's dreadful
Most kind and selfish
To have all from you.

You dance me
In the moonlight
Except we are not outdoors
But inside a hallow chapter.

You chance me
It's not luck
Pure goodness and enchantment
Your charm.

You make me
It's forsaken
A simple madness
From one to another.

You show me
Not the same
What you want to be
From what is all too real.

# BEST WITH MORE THAN ONE

I'm Krystin. I am a weight proportioned to height, hot body babe. I am blessed with pretty curved young breasts and a tight, toned round ass. I have short curly hair. I like my hair short because it's easier to maintain especially when you're as busy as I am. I am twenty-four and still get carded wherever I go. I take pride in keeping up with more than just appearances. I love my body, mind and whom I am. With a fair skin complexion, slender young body, long delicate tongue and face like a china doll, I almost get it all. Let's be honest, you can never have it all. I am independent meaning I support myself. With no parents or siblings to help or even get emotional support from, I had to learn to be independent at fourteen. Ten years later I live alone, I have a great job and don't have to answer to anyone. I enjoy my life, but lately there's been something missing. I have been bored for awhile now and I want more in my life.

I want sex. I realize that most people still don't talk about sex. Although sex is the most beautiful pleasurable act it's also the most taboo. To me, sex is a necessity, come on, we need it to evolve, without sex I wouldn't be here and neither would you. Without sex there'd be no war. Man feels the need for war to prove their power in other words their sex. Without sex, relationships won't survive at all. Needless to say, I love sex. I have had thirty-two sexual partners of which twenty-one are men. I don't think that makes me bisexual or freaky, I just have a great appreciation for sex and believe it or not there are millions like me. I like the way it feels when I come and no matter how many times I reach orgasm, it always feels superior to any other sensual experience. There's nothing else I know that compares to sex. I have been called a voyeur, an exhibitionist and even a nymphomaniac, but those are just words. They are descriptive words for a highly active sexual person. I don't want to describe my sex. I just do it whenever I want and however I want with whomever I want.

My favourite sexual moment is with both sexes. I love to suck a cock while another chick is tongue thrashing my dripping pussy. It's exciting to eat a woman's pussy while she is getting dicked in the ass. It's even more exciting when the dick is in her pussy. The smell is like nothing else in sex and the succulent taste of them both at the same time is bliss beyond sin. An older couple wanted me to join them and show them an enlivening time at a swingers club, so I did. I sucked up all her pussy juices, which smoothened my cracked winter lips while her husband rammed into me like a hungry bull. Barely half way into it, another couple joined us. Before I knew it, I was being satisfied in every way. I was on fours with two dicks in me, one in my throbbing pussy and another in my butt hole, and two slippery clits to lick up. Electrifying! Sweat was dripping from my neck to my lower back and navel. My body was delighted in every way, how invigorating it was.

Having good dick is getting your vagina banged so hard that the next day the inside of your thighs and the opening of your pussy are sore. Everybody likes it rough sometimes. To have someone else watch while I am being roughed up is even more gratifying. When I'm roughed up, I come harder and better. Just imagining that the person I'm with is saying wicked things and sexually pleasing me with a hand around my neck is enough to get me coming. Sex is good with one person, it's masturbation. It's better with another person because you can give fulfillment to each other. Sex is best with more than one partner at the same time. Picture him, her and I, the boundless possibilities to attain and surpass exhilarating orgasms.

---

## Beloved

like beloved, i'm pregnant
     with the desire to love you
     to be your love

i want to engorge myself
     with the salty taste of your ocean
     no cares to what others might say

standing naked, i hide nothing
     from your inquisitions about my
     past
     from your acquisitions of my
     presence

see, my eyes gulp you greedily, framing
details
     to mount you in the chamber of my
     heart
     like diamonds in Sethe's ears

unlike beloved, though, i don't plan to
vanish in my tracks
     'cause i'm gone wait you out, walk
     you down,
     be the stars in your crown

no, i ain't going home, back to Spirit,
without loving you, my love

## Bondage

What I know is
I don't know
Anything
About bondage,
Though submission
Directs me when you are
Present.

I cannot look full upon you.
You are The Sun,
Hot, a heat source,
A meteor.
Instead I want to lie under you,
Feel the intensity of your heat,
Take the moon rock you
Thrust into my open crater.

Where are your chains?  You know,
The ones that wrapped themselves
about
My heart the August evening
I first saw you
At a backyard barbecue,
A beer
Caught in your grip
Where I longed to be
Chained like keys to your hip.
You are my love letter
Evoking pink sighs and fuchsia moans,
Culled from
Surrender.

The touch of your hand
On the small of my back
Creates an arch
That locks me in position:
Your preferred view.

Welcome to "The Valley of the Siren."
Here.  This is the key
To your every fantasy.
I'll resist nothing,
Propose you do
What you will.
I consent,
I acquiesce,
Until you are supine between my thighs.

No.  I know nothing
Of S&M games
Or why someone would want
To be subdued.
But when you are near
Or your name creeps into
My space,
Scenes take shape:
Arrayed in black vinyl
Soft as leather,
I slip to my knees
Bow my head
Patiently awaiting
The jewelry that is your choke chain.
In deference,
I listen for your command
Compliance, I understand, in

Black stilettos
Poised to dance
Spread
strut,
A Fem Manifesto,
I am the answer to any question
You conjure.

Black lace at my breasts,
Crotch-less clit bejeweled,
My wrists you tie in an effort to
Make haste.             You can't wait.
You brand me with your breath,
Lock the door and
Toss the key to the floor.
And I whimper,
While you watch me hang from the
ceiling
My flesh pressed against thick nylon.
I am balled, exposed, no holes barred
Delirious for your pleasure.

Bound, I am your limo ride
And your driver.
Wrists cuffed in pink fluff,
Ankles clasped together
In licorice,
Edible undies sticky---
I will leave a masterpiece
Of hickies
Across the terrain
Of your plains.
From you,

I will bring punany rains
To rival
The monsoons of India
The Philippines
And Burma.
When our scenes dissolve in climax, I
will leave these stilettos,
My handcuffs,
For your senses to behold,
Until you return
To demand that climatic mix of
capitulation
And adulation,
The reasons why you came.

O the sweetness of Love's exchange.

## Fem Dreams

Hey, Boo
Yes you
with the perfect mix of boy in yo' gyrl
no frills, no curls,
You

Lend me your Being
for right Now
Listen with your soul, not your mind

I won't settle for less
my request your total presence
at best

Get it?

The past and future aside
look into my eyes
Tell me no lies

If you dwell in Truth
and She in you
you know it's nothing new

The right Fem touches the deepest part
of you
straight leaves you confused

Your emotions you hope she doesn't
abuse

seeing she's got your head in a flurry
you hurry
to see her stiletto stroll
into a room
tip toeing your pulse to panic mode
that heart on boom
especially if you know
she knows
no debates
the effect of the seismic flutters
on your heartscape

Your power of speech failed
the last time she
sashayed
across your slick  syrupy, slippery
fantasy
high steppin' and prissy
she dripping through your wet dreams
forming puddles in your consciousness
her reflection
lying soft and satiny atop your sheets
sweetness everywhere
The scene complete, it

got you stuck
on repeat

'Cause you don't know what to kiss
first
her smooth sexy feet
those cheeks, Oooooo those cheeks

have you hummmmming stupid
yummmmy tunes
about her tight crescent moons
dipped in a sepia glaze
her waist flat lining towards her cute
kitty
unthonged
you'll be crazy if you can't get a quick
taste
your tongue sprung
practically hurting
to be slurping her
Damn Fem about to crack your plate

Now you craving that—
Here…take the pen
you
fill it in
from start to finish
Just know she sooooo sugary
she throwing you in a diabetic haze
trying to recollect if ever there were
days
you said you'd never find pleasure
kissing whatever---

Here's the real deal
every molecular inch of you
seeks
her body heat
Big Gryl, quit it--admit it--
that Fem got you beat

But you poetically cool
a right proper butch
your bag near to take Miz Fem to
school
let her know whose rules she's abiding
while she's eyeing you
buckling up
tantalizing her with your tool
locked in place
a pat to its base
You betta know it…
No limp noodle can
keep your Fem
on ooze

No need for shame
you got game
you remind yourself
'cause
here she cums
the afterglow of her climax
thick on her trembling limbs
those sexy lashes fluttering
eyes rolled back
you got her stuttering
that appetizing mouth muttering
your name

And her pussy whines so pretty, it stops
Time
How about that?
Like a larger-than-life image on the big
screen
at the Imax

And she can send it back
nothing shady
about this Fem

Now she can get it, Lady

Natural curls spill across your neck and
her hot kisses bless
the skin you're in
kicking up a furor in your breasts
and then tap-kiss that stomach
where it
damn it---
parts those
thighs

And you can't remember the last time
you felt the power of the
Sublime
in the Now
your mind is like HOW can this Fem
be wiping out your memory bases
fucking up traces of the last baby gyrl
who
rocked your world

But you too cool, nobody's fool to let
go that quickly
even when the shakes
can't be faked

Until those heart-shaped lips
head south
fire in her mouth
kisses freezing your joints like the ice in
her hood
on her way to your "Head Lady in
Charge"
who knows when to bow
down
under the temperature of the right
Fem's licks


The flicks her tongue gives your clit
got you—
S      H      I      T!
holding sheets
head thrown back, pretence ended
eyelids suspended
holding
falling
cussing
clinging
calling her, let's say
tonight
hoping
praying
the number's right

'cause

Fem dreams alright
but
you can't wake
to another day
without
that Fabulous Fem Fantasy
by your side
in her place


**I Love You Like...**

a hot shower in the middle of the night
after i've kissed a trail of fire down
your belly and the sight
of you naked fills me with delight.

like a december thundershower pelting
a hypnotic melody
against my kitchen's windowpane,
while you, my penelope,
accept no other lover.
only for me, you wait patiently.

like a desire that dictates you want no
other
almost akin to the same intense love a
baby loves its mother
when just the smell of her flesh is better
than a cover.

like lovin' you fills me to the seams,
poppin' my stitches,
but i don't care if my britches
drag in the ditches, 'cause for your love
i'd walk down witches.

like, oh yeah, grabbing a bull horn
showing um even if this love they
scorn,
i'll not be afraid to face fear and be
reborn.

like the smell of freshly baked bread
that suffuses me when I sit between
your legs,
red and aflame with a passion that, in
some, evokes dread.

i love you like…like…i love the mango
taste of your lips
in the morning when you pull on those
baggy jeans and i lisp,
your beauty hard and soft at once,
putting a switch in my hips.

yes, i love you like all this…

## LOVE'S FREESTYLE

Song descended the softly illuminated winding staircase leading down into a darkened basement. A sleepy sigh slipped from her lips the second she glanced at her watch. With each step, she cloaked herself in a deliberate mindfulness. Although it was already 9:12 P.M., with another Friday morning looming, a persistent passion to sing warred with an annoying ache deep in her bones and won. It hadn't been an easy victory. From the moment her beige Escalade purred to a stop in her marked CEO parking designation at the marketing firm to the conclusion of an annual financial board meeting, she had been ready to do what she was doing right now.

No matter, though, she figured. It had been weeks since her mind allowed her to focus on the intention to spend more time in the basement she'd remodeled into a state-of-the-arts recording studio complete with the latest equipment and furnishings to advance her music career. Frankly, one day was entirely too long to be away from both of her passions: the woman whose memory she fled for most of her waking hours; the other singing, a passion for which she'd renamed herself.

Inside a sound booth the size of two rooms, she flipped a slew of switches and flooded the space with jazzy background music and stark, white light, immediately shrouding the outside hallway in an agreeable darkness. The press of other buttons vibrated the air with an undercurrent of hums and beats and a tract of her voice floating just above the wispy whirr of the air conditioner coming to life. She bowed her head in gratitude before inviting the presence of her inner genius and rifled through sheets of lyrics Afreeka, an underground artist, had written for her then quickly reviewed a sheaf of music she'd written in '06. Her first CD had to be mind-blowing, even if most of it was yet in her head, where it had been for so long she dated its conception with Cynthia's leaving.

Song released a long weary exhalation.

Everything she'd written in the past year wrapped itself in undertones of the 'Baby, come back blues.' Though her cousin, Triage, had been the only one brave enough to articulate the limbo that kept Song stuck in place like an insect on flypaper, she felt her boyz, musicians with whom she'd held jam sessions prior to the crash of her 10-year marriage, had let her down, one by one. How could they flat stop showing up for their weekly get-togethers, claiming Song was present bodily, though spiritually AWOL? The nerve of them. But when Cynt first left, to be honest, the studio went off-limits, and Song, with the whim to blame everybody outside of self, had begun burying her sorrow under added responsibilities at work not to feel Cynt's absence. She got so she abhorred that liquor-laced decision to know what it would feel like to fuck Joelle, a young sista who sometimes sang back-up for the group. Her desire to know if she could make Joelle holler deepened whenever Cynt withheld for too long. Later Song impugned that damn penchant of Cynt's to court late-night TV, which replaced their once on-and-poppin' midnight play. Hell, it had her still asking herself why one of her boyz or Triage didn't back her into a corner and splash water on her after-jam-session revelries that haloed her good reasoning, presenting the warped notion that a one-night tryst could be trusted to a club's back room, far from her wife's soft, scented embrace.

But shit. She had to drop the bullshit sooner than later. Fact was, she was wrong. No matter how she reasoned and seasoned it, her indiscretion led to the one sin Cynthia Renee Holliday could not abide: betrayal, and there was no one to charge but Song. Fuck sidestepping the reality that the longer they remained separate, the greater the more irreparable their vows. Yet she never ran from anything. Long.

Remembering where she was, Song noticed a guitar slumbering in a corner near the amplifier, stiff under a sprinkling of dust. When she reached for it, lifted it, studied it, cradled it, then opened a drawer under a marble countertop and retrieved a cloth, the instrument sighed. Something it hadn't done in next to forever. Could this woman who had fallen out of love with it be wiping its unpolished wood, fingering and tightening its neglected strings, thrumming stray melodies as she examined it, whispered to it? The guitar stretched in one long vibrating chord, and Song's deft fingers commanded it do her bidding. In a smooth, loving motion, months of desertion disappeared. Its night had finally arrived. She was positioning it on her warm, jean-clad lap, gently, nestling it between her thighs, making the kind of music she wanted to hear.

She and the guitar merged. Unfurled, her voice came true and astoundingly beautiful; melding harmoniously with the guitar's more haunting, plucked soulfulness. Together, woman and instrument crooned their passion for the one woman each adored—she Love, it her. The studio became their haven and recorded a saccharine angst both nurtured.

Eventually, when each had had enough, Song stopped and smeared thick beads of perspiration across her forehead, where the moisture had begun to trickle past her long lashes into her eyes, obscuring her vision. A good thing. So, too, the studio walls and mic sweated with an ignited fervor, a creamy, dreamy vibe having seeped into Song's soul, shaping itself into a whisper that teased her earlobes with an emotion for which she'd staved for months. It enticed her to return the guitar to its open, newly dusted case and hug herself for a minute. One minute. Instantly, gratitude bolted through her, streaking from head to toe, a synergy of chakra cleansing energy.

There would be no more trading truth for lies. No, it was going down tonight. In a significant way. And it didn't bother her she had no idea how.

Hours lapsed in a peaceful, musical solitude.

When thirst ravaged her throat, driving her to a floor-model refrigerator near a towering speaker, a parched Song withdrew bottled water and drank in long, greedy swallows. She was consumed in the throes of the power of music—like holy water--to heal, baptize, and communicate. Over near the hanging ceiling mic, her baby browns spotted a patient synthesizer ardently craving her tender, magical fingertips. Jealous, it couldn't understand Song's partiality for that damn Guitar now resting in its open case, still basking in the music it and Song had made.

To the synthesizer's amazement, its lover seated herself at the keyboard with cloth in hand. Once the dust had been lovingly dismissed, it nearly lost its legs when those fingers gracefully grazed its keys then hovered above the instrument, as though in reverential offering. Benediction style.

A switch flicked, and it hummed to life with a raspy awe.

From Song's throat, sounds trebled, lay themselves out on the currents of sighed emotion and vibrated the electric-blue studio air. Flood gates parted, and that voice poured out of her in a live freestyle of music and feeling. Desire. Angst. Regret. Enthrallment. She accepted it all. And the sheer delight of it morphed her fingers, until cage-less birds, they winged above the keys: diving, teasing, pressing, tapping, dancing, gliding.

Song closed her eyes and opened herself further to the Goddess doing her thing. Now one, they made a mad, bitter, engaging, soul-stirring piece of music, filling the studio with a nakedness that made her shiver from the roots of the silky dark curls caught in beads of wetness on her forehead and kitchen to the damp slickness behind the crotch of her Gap jeans. Melodious tension magnetized the soles of her well-worn house shoes, tapping time, to the hardwood. Gripping. Her shoulders and mid section rocked and heaved, the whole of her focused on expressing obsession for the two passions of her life--music and Love. Though trapped in a zone, Song gradually became more and more aware of two outlines beyond the glass; the tall one had to be Triage, her favorite cousin with a key and her own security code to Song's front door; the other probably a DJ groupie Triage had the tendency to attract wherever she worked the city's dyke dives.

"Damn, Cuz, what the deal? What got you wildin'?" A familiar chuckle came loud and clear over the studio's intercom, curling Song's lips in a chummy grin. "We been listening for a minute, in the doorway. Didn't wanna fuck-up your groove, 'cause damn, Song, that's the shit!" She stepped closer to the glass. "How long you been workin' on that number?"

Song got up and turned off the recording equipment. Her arms rose in a leisurely stretch above her head, while she took in Triage's mane of wild curls falling helter-skelter across her broad shoulders and back. That cousin of hers had the sort of rakish good looks women fell for, plunged in head first for, got bent out of shape and broken up for, whenever she intimated she needed her space. All hell broke loose under Triage's masterful hypnotism—baggy jeans, Bob Marley T, ball cap turned backwards; not to add, hypnotism in spite of a clipped attention span, loose hands, and looser eyes. Song shook her head. Mostly femmes, one or two straight women, some bi-sistahs, and a healthy mess of butches wreaked themselves to be near the woman.

"Just got in here tonight."

Triage winked. "It's morning now, Cuz. You callin' in?"

Song hunched her shoulders, noticing the face of the black and red, ceramic Bombay wall clock for the first time. 3:35 A.M.

The studio lights left a moist sheen on her face and under her arms. She backhanded her forehead and smeared the dampness through her hair, slicking it flat then walking into the hallway.

"What up, Tree?" Song's dark-brown gaze swept her cousin, whom she pulled into a bear hug, and then shifted to the shorter woman at Triage's side. A studious, unassuming sort. She didn't quite fit the Triage prototype, Song noted, so either she must be fucking or her cousin had met her match.

A head higher than Song, Triage folded her arms under breasts flattened with the artifice of a band and an exercise bra and jutted her chin towards the full-bottomed girl. "This Lita."

The girl's lips formed a sexy pout and began moving with a seemingly inadvertent economy of movement, forcing Song to lean forward, tuning her ear to make out the timber of a subdued, "Hi, nice to meet you." Appealing, she explored the hall's hardwood as if it was glass and she lost beneath it. Then, rather unexpectedly, she met Song's curiosity with a pretty smile. "I like your flow. You a showstoppa. Where do you perform?"

"Thanks. I'm here for right now." Song covered an escaping yawn in a quick palm. The gesture lost on the girl, she granted herself permission to launch into a full-blown expose on the merits of the jazz, hip hop and alternative venues around the city and the local talent with constant gigs, although, in her opinion, they weren't half the singer or instrumentalist she'd heard in Song's freestyle performance tonight. Her father, Lita announced, was a jazz giant living in Cuba. In Havana. "He's one of the famous Los Hermanos Hernandez," she beamed, scanning Song's amused face for a tad of recognition.

If Song weren't so tired, she might have listened to the enchanting Latina accent a while longer, but Triage went to clearing her throat, dang near rudely. The utterance lidded her girl's monologue instantly. "Lita's not the sole surprise this morning, Song."

Cool, Song thought, reaching for Lita's hand. A gentlewoman, her lips brushed the soft sepia skin. "When I gig, you got front row tickets."

The lips and promise tingly, Lita lowered her head, and lightening fast, Song landed a flash of punches on Triage's tattooed biceps. "I like this one, Cuz. Bring her again. Now what else you got?"

By way of answer, an alluring scent of African black soap with Shea butter and aloe arrested Song's attention. Making her sniff the air. Mmmmm. She drew in a lungful of the enticing aroma. Had she been alone, she might have licked the scent from the air, but instead, she settled for the few strides it took to clear the short hallway to her listening room, a beautiful space in which she critiqued music and meditated and, right now, the room paled surrounding a woman whom she'd renamed, when she renamed herself.

Song would know her scent anywhere.

'Hey, Love, how you doing? It's good to see you."

Just like that, she wasn't aware of much. Not her own breath. Triage escorting Lita out the way they had come. The wall clock's hands ticking tenaciously towards 5:41 A.M. Quite frankly, she didn't give a decent damn about anything outside of the way Love perched on the circular black leather sofa unit, all soft and sexy, comfortable, sandals tossed, rosy brown legs curled beneath her, in the whispered light of a hanging spider lamp.

Love rose upward, leaning toward Song, as if to cancel the whole four months she'd been away, proffering herself over the guitar-shaped glass coffee table. "Song." She murmured the name. 'Sooong." Exhaled it akin to the hushed sighs Song remembered those lips issuing at the end of a draining climax. "Your music is mesmerizing. Even more than I remember. I am speechless."

So was Song.

A bother to waste her energy on mere words, she decided her actions would freestyle all she'd longed to say to this woman for weeks now. Standing there, taking her in, questions swirled through her head. Where had Triage found her? What had they said to one another? Had she longed to return to her? And why tonight of all nights? How had she spent her days? Who had been loving her? The last question fucked with the elation in Love's eyes, and—poof--, none of the answers mattered. What mattered was her presence here and now.

Slowly, gratefully, Song inhaled her, cherishing again that unforgettable scent. She could smell it every day of her life. The rustle of the woman's olive green sundress broke her trance.

As if in a dream, she made her way to the sofa pit, pushed back the smooth-edged coffee table, and knelt before the only woman with the power to bring her to carpet, hardwood, grass, or gravel. She fixated on a pair of the most luscious lips she'd ever known. Love knew that stare. So, too, her tongue, a sliver of pink skimming bow cup lips, trailing a sweep of wetness.

Song stiffened.

The image sent a wave of fever to her clit. She'd seen Love moisten those lips in her dreams, where she'd done the same, licking them, tasting, teasing, and nipping Love's bottom lip. She sighed. Extended a hand to touch the perfumed perfection of pretty feet, naked legs, and silky thighs, smooth and brown except for a scar above the right knee. Song's fingertips heated Love's flesh and stroked her sundress upward, high and higher, then high enough to cup their goal: handfuls of voluptuous, intoxicating hips. No permission needed between them to do what she was doing, Song could see the havoc she was wreaking in Love's frenzied lashes and quivering limbs. Her hold caressed and tightened. Her fingertips photographed the texture of that glorious ass, unthonged, high and tight, thank goodness. Shit, she could have identified it blindfolded, with one hand tied behind her back.

Easing up from her kneeling position, Song anchored herself on the sofa and placed a knee between Love's legs, widening them. She lowered her face to the open, darker one to document the woman close-up, to reference the fragrance of her breath, to record that exquisite, full mouth with her own thinner, eager lips, to taste it before her cool fled.

When she took them, swallowing them with her own mouth, relishing their flavor, Song brushed every gentlewoman trait she'd ever cultivated aside and bunched the hem of the sundress around Love's waist so her scrutiny could detail what she'd wished with a longing that burned like heated steel. The quick movement left Love shivering, hands glued to Song's wrists, mouth open, her thighs spreading as she scooted her ass lower for Song's tongue to thrash, and caress, then dance, melting her until she dripped a sweet and sticky cream. The lickdown fierce, it fed one while welcoming the other. "Let me freestyle my gratitude to the stars for the gift of you on this miraculous morning."

Love's shoulders hunched at the seductive murmuring against her ear.

"Is that okay with you?" Song's persistent mouth caught and nibbled Love's, sharing her taste with a kiss. Her gentle licking generated a smoldering under Love's skin, pooling drops of perspiration along her curly hairline, across the top of her shoulders, in the palms of her hands, on the inside of her baby-soft thighs.

"Song." Love moaned the name. She choked on the wave of urgency creeping, tumbling, slipping, sliding, and then surging through her body like electricity. "I'm your song, baby. I will go wherever you take me. Sing me. I will master…whatever….tune…you play." Words fluttering, Love's thighs trembled under Song's massaging strokes and parted wider. To better anchor herself, she grabbed Song's sculpted forearms and submitted willingly as this woman, her woman, whose voice along could bring her to climax, spread her, to bring Love's pussy to her smile again and, staring up, took another lick but this time filling the sweet, juicy cunt and ass with force and rhythm.

The combination shut Love's eyes. Locked her thighs over Song's ears. Scooted her rounded ass damn near to the hardwood, and splayed her thighs affording Song more of an appetizing view she adored. If she could, Love would have unhinged herself, snakelike, for Song to have greater command of her assets. Together or apart, she went liquid for no other woman.

Song sucked her in greedily.

She stroked a melody of poetry within her, the music her fingers made pumping loud slurps, slick notes from her downy-topped lower lips, feverish fingers slipping in and out of Love's dew. With graceful skill, she blew the tender reed of Love's clit, while forming her fingers into a slow, steady fist that eased its way up, and up, deep into Love's ravished sweetness. Song's other hand plucked an enchanting refrain from Love's tighter, smaller pucker.

And Love followed her. Her body did its best, heaving and rippling, not to buck itself from its climactic connection with Song's lead. Her breasts rose and fell in a delicate groan of pleasure, leaving Love's mouth open and gasping for breath. Her nipples, chocolate tips of delight, begged for

Song's touch or tongue. Try as she might, though, she meant to attach herself to Song's biceps, to steady her ride, but her hands kept slipping and sliding, uncooperative, from the damp skin. One raked jagged lines through Song's slick black hair, glistening with perspiration. Another found its way into Song's warm mouth. Then both tugged again on the woman's arms, scratched her back, and dipped into Song's button-down shirt to caress her breasts.

Giving her all, Love followed Song over the skittering cadence of a jerky, visceral music that struck up a sigh from somewhere near her G spot. She trailed it straight past a riff of a bad beeline between her clit and her ass, slick with her honey, and just followed her clean to an explosive ejaculation that drenched Song's nose and lips and chin and cheeks. Song's tongue strained not to waste a single drop.

But this time the sight of Love's succulent, beautiful pussy paralyzed Song. When she could move again, she clenched Love's entrée of an ass and knew again a juice she never wanted to be without. Ever. And not just anybody's juice. Only this juice did it for her, got her crunk. "Damn, Love," she finally intoned when she could calm her own breathing well enough to speak, one cheek resting on Love's thigh, "yo' shit is so divine, so pure. Absolutely gratifying. Satisfying." She stood and plopped down on the sofa and pulled an exhausted Love onto her lap and slipped her sundress over her head.

Meanwhile, Love couldn't put two sentences together.

Kissing a queue of fire from Love's neck to her earlobes to the space between her shotgun breasts, Song wasn't in for speaking anyway, nor was she in for only one good go-around this delicious morning. She'd call in later. Yes, indeed. Yes, indeed. Right now, she had another verse of freestyle in her for this woman.

An epiphany hit her with a powerful blow. All she ever wanted to rip were Love's freestyles. That was the feeling waiting to beat its way to her surface earlier, she realized, in excitement. And damnit, there was nothing stopping her. Intent had brought her downstairs to the studio, to new music, and Triage had brought her Love.

Sucking candy nipples and salt from the curve of breasts, Song gripped the wet skin of Love's waist and fingered her belly button. She meant to kiss another mouth-watering gush from

Love's inner essence. Meant to feel Love's limber legs wrapped around her waist, later, after she'd climbed three flights of stairs to their bedroom, where she would massage Love and sing to her again and, much, much later, strap up to freestyle another unforgettable number neither would ever forget.

## I Wanna Fuck You But...


I don't wanna stay.
I just wanna love you when I'm ready
to play.
I make no promises, but you won't
complain.
You look so sweet;
I don't wanna ever see you in pain.

I wanna fuck you, but you must
understand.  You're special.
I don't just ask for everybody's hand.
I wanna fuck *you*, make *you* moan,
make *you* sigh.
I wanna take your kisses in the softest
drive-by.

Baby, you haven't known true fucking.
I can see it in your look.  Stop ducking!
Me?  I can look your knees weak.
My voice alone can render you unable
to speak.

C'mere.  Lay by my side.
I'm gonna kiss you until your fear
subsides.
Then I'll stroke you where it aches,
Make you shiver like you're standing in
a freezing lake.

I wanna fuck you, but all keys
I must possess.
None of you will be off-limits
when you I undress.
How else will I know how to fuck you
best?
Baby, believe me when I confess,
I'm unlike the rest.

I wanna fuck you any way I choose…
In the park, in my car, you can't loose.
I got climaxes for you alone.
I know a thousand and one ways to own
your moans.

Angel, I wanna fuck you, but you gotta
give it to me willing.
You're not a fuck thing,
and I don't do stealing.
When I touch your knees, I want your
juices coming down.
Love's perfume outta be rising high,
swirling round and round.

I want you on your knees
The back and front door open, begging,
"Please, baby, please."
You know you wanna be fucked, but
you also wanna relationship.
I say, "We are relating. Ours is the
ultimate companionship."

And on those occasions
when I wanna be fucked,
I want you to give it up;
I wanna feel sufficiently sucked.
I want you to spread yourself across me
like jam on toast.
I want to sizzle and sputter,
like a well-basted roast.

Let me say again, I do not boast.
I will stretch your legs from coast to
coast.
When you take your next breath to
breathe,
You will murmur my name and pray
I'm back before I leave.

So what's the deal?
Exercise your own will.

Speak your mind.
Leave other people's opinions behind.
Remember, if Society had her way,
You'd be single and lonely or married
and on layaway.

I wanna fuck you.
But you gotta wanna play.
And if not now,
I'll see you next time around.
Maybe then you'll be ready to get on
down.

## I Want to be Your Recipe

I want to be your recipe whenever you
cookin'.

When you gather flour, eggs and butter,
Milk, oil
and baking soda to stir into batter,
I can be the sugah
to make your batter matter.

I want to be your recipe
When you stir fry.
I'll be the onions to make you cry,
Then you can caramelize me
To add the sweet and sour to your
veggie melody.

I want to be your recipe
When you bake your dinner bread.
I'll be so still you can mold me,
knead me,
And jelly roll me
Into something delicious enough to take
to bed.

I want to be your recipe
When you slice apples for your pie.
I'll be the spice to lay across the top.
I'll be the oozing hot,
bubbly brown syrup.
I'll even be the cool whip dollop

To make your taste buds hollah.

I want to be your recipe
When you're blue
and tired of low-fat dishes.
I'll be your skillet of feel-good wishes.
Full of fat and carbohydrates,
I'll have you zonin'
Faster than your brain's release of
serotonin.

I want to be your recipe
When you spread your pizza dough.
You can toss me up and twirl me,
Make me dizzy,
Say, "I-I can't take anymore!"
But I'll wait patiently for your
pepperoni and cheese,
Then cover you in my spicy sauce,
Make YOU whisper, "Pleeeze!"

I want to be your recipe
When you boil your collards.
I'll be your hambone,
My flava creepin' through your pot,
Make you leave canned greens alone.
'Cause I'll straight terrorize your
cornbread, and make your lips my own.

I want to be your recipe
When you grill your steak.
I'll be your tenderizer,
Make you shiver and shake,

Shout, sizzle and sputter,
Rime and sign a thousand ways,
I can be your lover.

Cook me into your soul's casserole.

## Oil Change

Undress me, baby,
Sand blast my paint,
Until there ain't
Nothin' left for me to do but revv until I
cain't.

Lift my hood, Sweetness.
Smell my aroma.
Let your fingers be my therapy.
Touch me between the nuts and bolts
others can't see,
And listen while my engine runs free.

Diana sang it; I'm sayin' it:
        "Come see about me."
No other mechanic will do.
It's true!
Nobody else knows the contents of this
trunk like you.

Close the shop.  Flip the sign.
Take me up on your lift.
I won't flinch, so lay on your back,
take out your wrench
And oil my engine until I'm drenched.

I'm a BENTLEY - the top of the line,
So tantalizing my bumpers alone leave
folks blind;
But you, you got me stuck on whine,

> For YoUr oil change
> I'll CuM every time…

## Midnight Phone Call

my cell calls your number
by heart, when midnight
fireworks spark a bushfire
between my legs, and the
clarkston sky is ablaze with
a purple ardor.  if you come, if
you stay, I will postpone
the day.

## Shall I?

Shall I kiss your tummy…
While my greedy hands cherish the
succulent curves
They deserve
As my lips sip
Your wine?

*Wait?  For whose sake?*
*Theirs or mine?*

Listen…if your Time were mine…
We'd live my will
And I'd steal or kill
To lie at your feet
My heart encased in bands of steel.

*Huh?  Why should I care who hears?*

Shall I nip your other licorice lips…
Let my delirious fingertips
Trip
Up the back of your tender thighs
To revel in the glory of your hips?

*What do I think they think?*
*Don't know.  Gotta get myself in sync.*

Shall I taste the nectar pooled in the
salty beads…
Between your candy breasts or sample

The raisin-nipples sitting high on your
chest---

*Do you always protest?  What pools?*

You know, the dew you brew in the
valley of your navel
And the tides you hide
Oooozing beneath your clit's sheathed
pride.

*Shhhhhhhhh.*
*Why deny your desire's ire?*

Lend me your feet, my precious
sweet...
Shall I kiss them till you weep?
Shall I suck each toe until your moans
shred the sheets?

*Have I lost my mind?*
*Hmmmmmm.  Possibly.*

Yeah...so recline and let me
voraciously dine
On your beauty's sublime
Else Time will leave us behind
If we deny this moment, this present,
And malign,
A love that binds.

*Day um!  I'll get it right this time.*

Shall we…
Put all else to rest
And wreak the super-structure of hell
Downright swear the world to tell
What it will and where…cuz…

I'm the zeal in your squeals, Baby
You're the swell in my yells, Mami

Fah real…
So here's the sealed deal…

Fuck um.

I shall and I will.

## The Power of the Pussy
(for Cee)

Whisper it?
I can't.
It's a truth that pants.
Be
Silenced?
Fat chance.

There are those
Who already know---
But will call you a hussy
If you boast---
The Power of the Pussy.

Think I lie?
Then let the truth testify.

Stocks skyrocket
And surpass lucrative money markets,
If virgin pussy
Unlocks money pockets.

Some folks will pay
To savor the display
Of pierced pussy.

It'll close your eyes
With the dollars they'll ply
On her thigh
Just to see her shake
And make the pussy purr

At the edge of the stage
Where somebody in the way
Will cause a rage.

Got pussy?
You can wage
War.
Ask Menelaus.
Men plotted from far and wide
To knock him aside.
Don't think it was only Helen's face
That wrecked his space.

Mark Anthony
Rowed for weeks
To see for himself how
Cleopatra's pussy
Made Egypt
A nation of
Prodigies.

Petting
The wrong pussy
Can leave you
Fucked up
Outta bucks
Minus luck
Yo' Wife chucked.

Shucks,
A pussy-whipped man
Is known by the gaping hole
In his nose,

I suppose.  And another
Woman couldn't take him
If her repose
Worked around the clock
Like Nodose.

Richard Pryor
Made you laugh
When he held the door for
His woman, then asked,
"Please
Leave
The pussy."

Some claim pussy
Is more powerful
Than any force
On this planet,
Outside
Of
The Divine.
Say it can render
One blind,
Deranged,
And
Confined,
If
The pussy was
Once plentiful
Then
Subsidized.

Wait.

Some straight women quake,
Say, "Let there be no mistake---
I ain't trying to get
Acquainted with pussy
No kind of way,
If Dick
Ain't somewhere in it."

Then, too, some bi-women
Gotta get
A lick before they even think to
Savor the flavor of the stick.

I'm told
Pussy can stack
Funny money,
Make a mean man
As sweet as honey,
Bring the White House
To its knees,
Make international leaders
As vulnerable as
Little boys sipping
Salt peter,
Vandalize the pillars
Of the Vatican,
And unleash mutiny in
Perfect unions, if pretty pussy
Parts its knees.

Handsome pussy
Can make
Femme pussy

Yowl,
Cough fur balls, and meow,
When they trot in their
Classic Dom
Style.

Look, if you snooze
And fall in love
With gold-digging pussy,
You'll cry the Blues
Before she's through
Spending your money
From Monday to Sunday.

So recognize
Understand and harmonize
To the tune of The Truth when it's
vocalized.

The Power of the Pussy,
I'm convinced,
Can't be circumvented.
Thus, respect it
Or be rent.

# LONGING FOR GEM

"Pussy is my only vice," she riffs, her voice a gravelly blues song, its melody as elusive as breath. I listen wholly consumed, the cell so close to my ear, it hurts. If I could smell her voice coming like wreaths of smoke through the phone, it would be laced with the sweet, hypnotic scent of weed.

My noon housecleaning suspended, I walk into the living room and slip to the beige carpet in a pool of summer sunshine. When she calls, I do little else.

Her honeyed voice drips inside me, forming amber trinkets I deposit in my heart's jewelry box. There is nothing I would not give to love and be loved by her. For a fleeting second, I probe her admission, wondering: is she owning a vice or hiding commitment issues? Whichever doesn't concern me at present.

Right now, I'm staring hard into the glassed doors of my living room fireplace. In seconds, I imagine her kicked back in her favorite arm chair, smoking. A loner, she only succumbs to the desire to talk at certain moments. When the silence of her apartment is overwhelming, and the woodsy beauty of her back porch favors a jail, and she figures I ought to have missed her enough to draw blood, and her front door isn't opening to a wood nymph come in to be fucked, she calls me.

While her pussy monologue is a potent aphrodisiac, the effect of her voice on my erogenous zones is what drives me insane, slowly, and brings me face-to-face with an irrevocable truth: *this woman does it for me.* No one before her has taken me to the brink of total distraction on the sheer essence of voice alone. Damnit. Every word she whispers burns me with a yearning for her touch.

I keep wondering how the hell this can be, though. The funny part is, I don't really *know* her.

"Pussy can rule the world if women knew their wealth," she growls, and then sighs wistfully, "but the knowing means little, if they know nothing of managerial skills. Anybody who recognizes pussy can quench thirst and satisfy hunger and multiply dollars can run shit."

I catch my thoughts then, and my breath, but it is too late.

In a glistening sweat as cold as diamonds, my own pussy loses its mind. Pining, weeping and shouting. It craves more than the meager stimulation it's getting from my fingers; no, it's demanding the heat of her breath and the arrogance of her boldness; desiring her thrusting, dipping, swirling, pumping fingers.

Surely, she knows.

I am much more than her dutiful ear.

I am the woman to whom she belongs.

If Eve Ensler had posed her controversial query to me when she penned "The Vagina Monologues," I'd have, before this second, characterized my pussy in one word: Gentility. Where certain pussies bitch and moan about what some woman does or does not do, mine cultivates the art of refined silence and manners. Yes, there are occasions it hungers for nothing more than to stamp its stilettos and paint a picture in magnetic shades of Jacob Lawrence reds and purples and yellows across the canvas of a wild woman's fingers, but it doesn't. Too discreet to pitch a fit. Too ladylike to hollah aloud. But that was then. Now I am training my pussy to shout. Attitudinally. No more genteel begging projected towards this woman taking what is left of my Saturday afternoon.

Gem's speech has slipped into wispy tones. Voicing what sounds like an apology, almost as if she is imploring me to put judgment in the garage with the garbage, before she shows up at my front door, one night soon, when her car will require a midnight spin.

Outside, the hum of passing cars and wafting chatter drift up into the treetops over my second-floor balcony to hang whimsically like rowed butterflies.

"Pussy is the world's universal language. A common denominator, if you will, to every people. Some women understand its semantics, and when they don't, they pretend it's as tainted as blood money. If pussy were dice in a crap game and women the sole players, most wouldn't take a turn. It's amazing, but some got that much self-hate." Her chuckles wash over me like balm.

I quiver.

For the longest minute, I forget my vow of boldness and wonder if she can hear it.

She has to hear it, my quivering. She must hear it splintering her perfect pauses. Pauses so exact, they scream. In the darkening living room, I cradle myself. Close my eyes and will her to cease being a disembodied voice in my ear and become a curious hand on my thigh.

When she is fed up with the silence, her voice comes an octave lower than the laughing children riding bikes on the road behind the house. "Men understand and practice the hell outta the crap game, never missing a turn. With everything, they connive to finagle someone else's turn, the game being what it is—a love affair with life. Therefore, I long for nothing. I wait for whatever to come around for me, in the dice. See, some people get pissed off with themselves, when the dots don't configure the number they want. The first time this happens, somebody wants to control, and consequently, the player who gets the pleasure of being controlled is a woman. Thus, it begins...the struggle to commandeer the pussy." She speaks as if she has given serious thought to the matter.

I feel more than I listen, enraptured.

There on the beige carpet, amongst back issues of O, *Essence,* and *Black Issues Book Review* and candles, I am afloat on waves thick with the aroma of honey. She's a pro, this woman. She's *got* it: the power to reach through the phone and strum me, pluck me, until I lie across her imaginary lap-- a busted guitar. Streaks of amber escape my shorts and sweeten one thigh.

I touch myself, rubbing the wetness into my clit. My nipples whine, begging me to say something, anything to elicit the music of her voice. When I don't, I appease myself with quick strokes of my thumb.

At that moment, I wish she could smell my headiness on our wireless currents. Had she, she'd have known. Her pussy proselytizing might have been saved for another audience requiring the benefit of debate. Me. I'm convinced, though pussy, my girl Cassandra swears, shouldn't dictate every conversation Gem and I share.

This once, I agree.

The next interaction I have with Gem Cochrane will be of minimal talk. On pussy or any other topic. The dice, I'm positive, will one day total jackpot, because I, too, know how to wait; my turn will come back around. And when it does, I will take my shot.

**\*\*\*\***

*Gem Cochrane*. She has been a haunting refrain in my mind for weeks. Yet I do not bow to my daydreams, not to fall apart on the rocks of her indifference.

One Sunday, Cassandra, accustomed to my setting her ears aflame with word of Gem and what she says and how much I want her, calls, hoping to get the dirt on my reticence. I give her nothing, and she offers a late lunch.

Miss Ena's is fairly quiet. We miss the after-church traffic of Jamaicans and locals by thirty minutes.

Once seated, Cassandra orders ackee, red beans, and jerk chicken. Opal, my favorite waitress, and I exchange small talk, and then I order my usual: cabbage, cornbread and ox tails in a sea of gravy.

"Why you so closed mouthed lately? Like you put yourself on Mount Pleasant's sick-and-shut-in list." Cassandra leans across the table close enough to cross my eyes. "She give you some?"

I shake my head in a flurry of auburn locs. "Listen to you. For someone who takes offense to pussy conversations, you sure have similar thoughts in your mouth on the regular."

Cassandra frowns like she's spotted her last boyfriend.

"Stephanie Young, don't play with me. Either you've met a new woman or that damn Gem finally retired her Mack Mama persona and gave a sistuh some lovin'. Now which is it, girlfriend?" She toys with the napkin-rolled silverware and condiments in the middle of the table. "Personally, I'm praying it's the first. That doggone woman with her brother's name, however cute she is, gets on my last nerve. If you weren't so strung out, you'd see Gem," she frowns again, smirking, "for the zirconium she really is and let the heifer ring until Doomsday." She laughs at her own wordplay before she regains her anger and deadpans, "Shoot, do the bitch-be-busy number on her behind. Be so busy the next time she calls, she'll break down and ask the Universe if your ass is still in town. Humph, she isn't the only beautiful butch in the ATL."

"Cassandra, you simply don—"

"And I don't want to know. If it were me, I wouldn't have a man who strings me along, calling me when he darn well pleases. I counted once. The slut waited three weeks and two days before she called you. Do you know how much living I do in that amount of time? I've gone through at least a man and a half, and you're still stuck on the prayer Gem Cochrane will call one more time." Cassandra's emotions throb fiercely behind a thin veneer of a smile.

"Sweetheart, I know what you're saying, but I haven't been sitting home waiting by the phone."

She's glaring at me, arms crossed, watching the words cloud my face. "Lies don't become you, girlfriend."

"Okay," I say, dropping my head. "So I'm sorry already."

Opal and our platter of mouthwatering food buy the time I need to think about how I'll word what's going on in my head. For twenty minutes we eat in a stilted silence, licking everything but the napkins. Finally, Cassandra raises one brow, and I know it's my cue to speak.

"I'm waiting, but I'm not waiting."

Cassandra's mouth jerks to one side comically. Then her lips pooch.

"What's that like...I ate, but I didn't eat?"

We fall out laughing.

"You could say that," I own. "Anything I say now will sound ironic, so I'll be quiet till I have something more exact to say. Good enough?"

Cassandra agrees, and then beckons Opal over to pay the bill.

\*\*\*

Cool water trickles through my locs, draining my mind of the day's details. The spray feels like heaven. I will not fret about the unwritten memos on my desk at work, I tell myself. I will enjoy this moment.

After I step out of the shower and wrap my body and locs in plush white towels, I recline across my bed, satisfied. Just back from the gym on a Friday evening, my muscles inhale Heather Headley's new CD in the softly glowing, vanilla-scented, yellow air of my bedroom. On the dresser, an arrangement of white roses, a gift to myself, adds another layer of romance to the scene, and I close my eyes, loving me for me.

The ring of my cell slices the ambiance no sooner than I drift off in a serene mindlessness. A nudging whim suggests I let it ring. Another urges me to roll over.

I stare at the name on the ID screen. It can't be, could it? Not after almost a month.

Gem.

Spoken or seen, the name does what it always does: *takes my breath away*.

"Good evening," I murmur, silky soft.

"What's good about it?"

What could possibly be bad about it? I think, if she dialed my number. Instead of flippantly admitting that, my tongue stumbles. Damn her. An instant smoldering has already begun to moisten the surface of my skin. My lips part, as do my thighs, while my eyelids slide downward in a feeble attempt to stifle every image outside of her voice.

"Hey, Stephanie. Don't leave a sista hanging. Answer my question."

Silence.

"What? Is that a difficult question?"

"What's good about the night?" I echo.

"Daaaaah?"

"You."

The uncharacteristic directness catches her off guard. In an uneasy pause, I sense her present enough to feel me smile. And I grin slowly, slyly, and then whisper softly, "That too difficult?"

"I'm downstairs."

"I'm upstairs."

"I know. I see your light. Wanna let me in?"

I deep breathe to anchor myself. "Maybe. But I'm unaccustomed to entertaining strangers at midnight."

"Me, too. After tonight, that won't be our concern."

The stairs seem to go on forever. All the way down, I remind myself to be cool. Not go gah-gah, like a starry-eyed teenager. She's just a woman. She pulls her pants on one leg at a time, I remind myself, remembering my daddy's favorite expression. Then another thought, "Confidence is sexy," resonating from an ESSENCE article, pops into my head and further buoys my spirit.

"Hi," she says, looking like a Girl Jock centerfold when I open the door. "How are you?"

"Great," I sigh, on slow simmer.

Somehow she realizes she could have been speaking Hebrew in the way I smile and reach for her hand. I didn't care that she could see my only concern pivoted on how fast I could get her upstairs and out of her clothes. For all her pussy talk, it's a miracle I never took Cassandra's bad-gyrl suggestion and threw myself across the chick's doorstep months ago.

Upstairs, thirty minutes later, Gem is naked on my bed, and the view is gorgeous. She is the type that renders me foolish. All testosterone and attitude. Thick locs and soft smiles. Rough hands and tender eyes. The woman is an onyx nestled in my white satin sheets.

I'm weak just looking at her.

But she will never know. This is my shot and I am taking it.

I go into action like a top-flight dominatrix at Club Venus. From my bureau's bottom drawer, I pull scented candles that, when melted, become massage oils and a white silk scarf. Out, also, come a matching white net top and leggings. "Damn, just talking to you, I didn't know you had this in you." Gem laughs and fluffs large white pillows at her back. "Should I be afraid?" She shudders in mock apprehension then cracks up, running one hand down her defined abdomen. Defiant, she lies in the center of the bed, studying me. Were she a cartoon, her thoughts would read: *You wanna play on my playground, Little Girl, play. Just don't waste my time. I'm here by design.*

So I return my repartee in a saucy stare: *Darling, I'm going to take so much of you, you'll have to move in to find yourself.*

At the foot of the king-sized bed, I slip my feet into the clear plastic heels I put there in hopes of a night such as this. Then I drop my towels and pirouette slowly, giving her full exposure to my perky breasts and rounded ass. This time she is the one gasping when I bend over, showing off my pretty pussy while stepping into the white, crotch-less net number and adjusting it to my curves in the large bedroom mirror.

Behind me, Gem's talk fizzles like flat beer. The whispering light of three candles flares up to take its place. Under an amber luminosity, I move to Heather Headley's magic, shaking my butt stripper sexy.

After two more dances, I lean over the bed, drip warm aromatic wax into my palms, and lift her feet one at a time. My gentle stroking eases her tension and stays any remaining boasts. Gradually, she loosens up, as my massaging commands her ankles, legs and thighs. With each stroke, Gem's piquant pussy stimulates my nose, and I want to testify: "Here lies a patch of paradise! Look and envy!"

More tantalizing wax and I by-pass her paradise, but not before I plant more kisses up and down her thighs, for a game of hide-and-seek, later.

"Are you alright?" I ask her.

Gem's hands on my breasts say what her lips can't.

I massage her abs then, kissing and caressing the taut skin. The clean scents of soap and summer cling to the tip of my nose. I nip and tease her, sense her body dancing under my tongue. Her thighs open and close below my butt, and I figure she's about to handle me soon, so I lower myself on her breasts and give her throat my undivided attention. Then I grasp her wrists, lift them over her head and tie them together. While her eyes caress me, I witness something inside her yield. It is her gift to me...her submission.

The dark-chocolate of her nipples melts in my mouth. Their taste makes me wage all-out war against them, making them stand and salute me and moan my name and rise and fall in a frenzied rhythm. She is responsive, uninhibited. So I explore her freely, thankful she is not hung up on "not being touched," as my tongue tats the tender flesh under her arms and around her sensitive earlobes with unmistakable Stephanie Young kisses. Against my ear, her breathing comes jarred and low. With candlelight framing her face, she stares into my eyes, hypnotized, until my falling locs swallow her view.

I do it then. Flat take her kisses, femme smooth.

She doesn't move, appears to have stopped breathing.

To test her pulse, I kiss her lips so imperceptibly soft…she flinches. The taste is delicious, just as I anticipate her southern pair will be. I lick her mouth and outline its shape with the tip of my tongue. A mouth this sensual has to experience my particular brand of lip gloss. She kisses me back hungrily. And I take full control, tonguing her mouth hard and fast. French kisses communicate my longing for her in the four months, two weeks and three days of not making love to her in the interim of our first telephone call.

My pussy somersaults and balances itself on a high beam of passion. Ecstatic. Its nectar soaks the white net of my leggings and flavors the air. Gem's mouth opens wide to taste me, her lower body bucking, lifting both of us off the bed in a tearfully slow grind.

Suddenly, a vision of us fucking strips the room of all sounds. In silence, my fingers blindly search for the white silk scarf.

Finding it, I tie her hands loosely above her head. Stroke her thick black locs and hover over her ear to whisper two commands: "Do not move. And do not touch me." To make it stick, I sigh a lingering, "Pleeease." Her body relaxes, becomes obedient, so obedient I part her thighs and make myself at home between them. My fingers automatically reach up to knead her breasts, as my lips joyously forage the joys of her wilderness: the tantalizing plateau of her middle, the savory savannah of sweet places under her breasts, even the region just above the property line of her woodland, warm and succulent, right under the equator of her navel.

I am engorged with her flavors, my body alive with her nearness and scent. Sensing my excitement, her thighs spread wider, inviting me to enjoy a respite and the exclusivity of her beauty, a long-awaited conquest.

All at once, I remember her bound arms and massage them with blissful strokes. This Amazon must be comfortable for my exploration of her treasures. A love bite on my right nipple is her thanks, my shock. The deed sends a charge to my pussy, threatening to topple it from its high beam. Struggling to balance itself, it fights like hell to keep from falling. Meanwhile, I continue my expedition into her heartland.

"Hmmm. Yeah."

Her moans rock me. Encourage me to search her underbrush for lost kisses with a greedy urgency. Gazing into her dark eyes, I lay claim to her like she belongs to me; kissing and tonguing, slipping and sliding, swimming and deep-sea diving in her ocean.

She is luscious, just as she is in my dreams.

Gem goes back on her former, cocky promise. Though I empathize, I offer no support.

"Wait, baby," she moans. "Oh, yeah. Yeah."

She's wiggling against her silky entrapment as though to break free at any minute so I do as I please; and, eventually, I spot them. My lost kisses. A touch on her thighs and she understands. Boundless, I want all of her. I bury my face in her, head moving sensually from side to side, taking what I have waited so long to own, taking her like no other woman existed before me, like no other woman will exist after me. And her pussy welcomes me in appreciation.

When she begins to quake uncontrollably under my registered tongue and presses the back of my head into her body, I nip and lick her until tremors drive her to pin me motionless between her powerful thighs.

"Sorry, baby," she apologizes later, cradling me close to her beating chest. "Blame it on the pussy. With you in my face, up close and personal, how was I to keep that whack promise not to move or to touch you?" Gem's laugh and kisses rain on my face, and I almost cry under her tenderness.

She props herself on one elbow. "Tell you what, though."

I snuggle into her side, all ears.

"How about I make it up to you over poetry and a snack?"

"A snack?"

"Yeah. At my place."

"Okay," I say, and then add, "Whose poetry?"

She frowns. "Mine. Sound like a winner?"

"Not if you run this same game on all your ladies," I purr, arms folded under my breasts. "Since pussy is your *only* vice...right?"

A sheepish smile crosses her face. "Hmmm. I wonder if I was just talking, ya know, to have something to say?"

My smirk advises her to can it, and she chuckles.

"Okay. Shock effect wins out every time. Tell me something that bizarre didn't have you wondering where I was coming from? Your curiosity and my sex appeal had you on hold, huh?" She scratches long, leisurely lines down her chest. "I had you on ice, stuck like a duck, baby gyrl."

I nod, giving her a *Yeah, right* look. "I thought you nuts actually. Let's say, I was too polite to not answer the phone. But your voice saved you."

We both smirk, simultaneously.

"Wrong," she quips. "You were smitten. Own it. I could have said hair was my vice and you would have followed my nutty musings to their end." She grinned, more cocky than ever. "You were praying I materialized at the end of the rainbow. Admit it."

Her sexy smugness pierces me and I toss a pillow at her but she ducks and fires two back.

"That is not true!" I scream giggle. "Don't fool yourself, Miss Testosterone. You have no influence up in this Hard Hat District."

Gem snatches another pillow and tosses it into the air over my head. It bounces off the wall and topples to the carpet. Our premier pillow fight jumps off amidst wild laughter with me falling off the bed and her helping me up from the carpet just to tickle me and watch me slip to the floor again. When Gem glances at the clock at two a.m., she ceases the play and lets me sample her confidence.

She beckons me to her with a commanding forefinger, and I crawl obediently to the center of the bed, where her hand on my waist excites me to no end.

"Ma'am," Gem sighs hotly into the hollow of my neck, "who operates this Hard Hat District?"

I mumble what I believe to be my name. Though it could have been hers.

"Is she available?"

"Al…ways," I stammer.

She begins licking my collarbone with abandon, her words inviting. "I need to confer with her. It's very important." Adding pure arrogance to the mix, Gem lowers those sensual lips to my right earlobe and starts a gentle, steamy sucking I'd promise her the world not to stop.

"Our closed-door, weekend conference will take place at my home. This weekend. Is your calendar free?"

"Yeah. Yes. Of course."

"Perfect. Let's go, Miss Young," she coos, slapping my butt and leaving her sting and palm there for a minute. "We got engagements to keep before we sleep, Sweet Pea." She disconnects and eases slowly towards the edge of the bed.

I suck my teeth, marshal what's left of my suspect confidence, and lean back against the pillows. "Give me some more of those gourmet kisses to get up for, Miss Cochrane."

"Later," she promises, rising up from the bed--tall, dark and stunning.

Damn! Her beautiful backdoor view rivals her kisses, as she swaggers to the shower sexy enough to make my body tremble. I am speechless watching muscles ripple across her back like waves. Ass rock solid, thighs sculpted, skin flawless—her beauty makes me bite my lip not to beg her back to bed.

Jackpot! I muse abruptly, giggling and rolling amongst the pillows anew. When the sound of running water interrupts my glee, I reach for the charged cell on the night stand beside my bed, and my finger can't dial Cassandra's house line fast enough.

## Tune Up

Can I get a tune up?
Like hot fries in ketchup?
Like the smart kid with her hand up?
Like a sista so fine, you don't care if
she's stuck up?
Like some jerk in traffic got yo' middle
finger up?
Like a Reese's peanut butter cup,
I'll make you lick me until yo' tongue
gives up.
So waz up?
I repeat.

Can I get a tune up?
You gotta eat.
Don't make me stand up?
If I do, parts of you, too, will rise up
Like a Million Men who stood up.
Like yo' Boo, who got yo' dandruff up.
Like a skirt so high, the sidewalk got up
Hit you between the eyes
had you lookin' up
To count daylight stars  yo' blood
pressure up.
Let me make this clear: I'm here and I
never give up.

Just lay down while I sit up
Like a revolution tearing down
to build up.
Like rent and taxes goin' up and up.

Like chocolate and vanilla swirled up.
Like the ocean, I'll never dry up.
So what about my tune up?
Blow on my neck.
Make my hair stand up.
You do and
I'll moan till the sun comes up.
"Everybody, shut up!"
Can't ya'll see my baby's got my
temperature                    up?

## Thank You

These poems and stories are
dedicated to Love's passion.
Erotica.  There is absolutely no
emotion like love that can bring
forth every other emotion.  To
my sister who has always been my
true friend.  There is not a
Hill that we cannot climb
together and stand on top in
great accomplishment.  I love
you.  To my girlfriends who
believed in me no matter what
and supported me without
reservations.  I am Frankly
blessed to have been Granted
your friendships.  Thank you
with love.  To my parents who
had me and to my mother who gave
me more than all I needed.  I
love and appreciate you.  To
understanding the difference
between a first love, a once in
a lifetime love and a true love
which I realized at the break of
Dawn.  To Rene with love for
finding Lulu.  To you, for your
support and feedback.  Merci
Beaucoup!

Appreciative love,
Gia Bella

Check out more poems and stories
online and submit some of your work.

## www.Gietic.com

Giselle is Poetic
Gia Bella is Erotic